CAREER FOCUS CANADA: A PERSONAL JOB SEARCH GUIDE, Second Edition

Helene Martucci Lamarre

Karen McClughan
Lambton College

D1315632

Prentice
Hall

Toronto

Canadian Cataloguing in Publication Data

Martucci, Lamarre, Helene
Career focus Canada : a personal job search guide

2nd ed.
Includes index.
ISBN 0-13-090829-0

1. Job hunting—Canada. I. McClughan, Karen, 1956-   . II. Title.

HF5382.75.C3M37 2001   650.14'0971   C00-932809-2

ISBN 0-13-090829-0

Vice President, Editorial Director: Michael Young
Editor-in-Chief: David Stover
Acquisitions Editor: Sophia Fortier
Marketing Manager: Sharon Loeb
Associate Editors: Susan Ratkaj and Meaghan Eley
Production Editor: Susan Adlam
Copy Editor: Alex Moore
Production Coordinator: Peggy Brown
Page Layout: Janette Thompson (Jansom)
Art Direction: Julia Hall
Cover Design: Amy Harnden
Cover Image: Photonica

3 4 5   05 04 03 02

Printed and bound in Canada.

CONTENTS

PREFACE

Welcome to the world of personal development and career planning! With the help of this book, you can create the tools you need for a successful job search in this competitive and often complex world. You will be able to think about, write down, and get into clearer focus your ideas on yourself, your career, and your goals for the future. Through the use of self-assessment techniques, sound career development theory, and individual application, you will be able to successfully get your first professional position, begin a new career, or change positions.

Who Should Use This Book?
Career Focus Canada: A Personal Job Search Guide is a useful source for everyone. It can serve as a textbook for college or university professional career development courses. It can be a valuable resource to individuals who are reassessing their careers or the effectiveness of current job search strategies. It can be a welcome companion for recent post-secondary school graduates who need to make some sense of the job market into which they are about to enter. Anyone who wishes to gain a competitive edge in the employment world will benefit from this book.

For Students: How to Use This Book
Use it actively. Don't just read the words; think about them. React to ideas, challenge your current ways of thinking, and energize yourself while you spend time with this book. As you think about how to use this guide most effectively, you may focus on particular areas such as résumé writing or researching companies. You may want to study the information and suggestions chapter by chapter to provide a comprehensive guide to successful job searching and career planning. No matter what the approach, you'll benefit from the experience.

For Instructors: How to Teach Using This Book
Career Development has been one of the most exciting and practical courses we have ever taught. Teaching from this text can be enjoyable and easy for you. Objectives are listed at the beginning of each chapter, along with questions for review or discussion at the end. While working with the text, encourage students to show their own experiences in job searching. The more the students can relate to the text, the more memorable and meaningful the course will become.

Changes for the Canadian Edition
Although we live and work in an increasingly global economy, there remain important differences between the United States and Canadian job markets. This Second Canadian Edition of *Career Focus*—now retitled *Career Focus Canada*—reflects those differences and includes valuable Canadian job search resources.

DEDICATION

I would like to dedicate this book to my husband, Tony Lamarre, for all his talents, patience, understanding, and support; and to my son, Ryan Lamarre for his love and faith in me.

Two more special people I need to acknowledge are my sisters: Marlene Norausky and Carol Smith. They are my mirrors into myself, my inspiration, and my dearest friends.

Finally, I want to recognize three of my very best canine friends: Pepper, for her longevity and companionship; Tara, for her energy and loyalty; and my very dear Muffin for her gentleness, love, and great courage.

—HML

I am honoured to have the opportunity to update this text for the Canadian marketplace.

I would like to dedicate my participation in this text to the students that I have had the pleasure to work with. I hope I have contributed in a small way to your career success. May you all achieve your goals and dreams!

Karen McClughan

1 INTRODUCTION:

The First Steps

There are many things to consider as you take the first steps of the most important journey of your career. A chart of the steps in a typical job search is shown on the next page. Questions about yourself are given in a self assessment chapter. The answers to these questions will help you decide what type of position and work environment are best for you. You will learn about the special skills and qualifications you bring to any position and company, and the different types of résumés you have to choose from when deciding how to market yourself in the best light.

As you read this book, you will discover how to select the best people as references, learn about the letters that are an important part of any job search, and receive some tips on filling out job applications. Next is a very thorough section on the importance and techniques of researching companies. Included in this discussion are ways to use timesaving electronic means to learn more about potential employers. Ideas on networking, including how to telemarket yourself and advice on attending career fairs, follow.

The types, forms, and basics of interviewing are given, including a review of typical interview questions, how to score in interviews with proof stories, and advice on how to negotiate salary and benefits. This chapter provides a strong base from which to gain confidence in your ability to interview effectively. You will be given some important tips on tests you may face as part of the interview process, as well as specifics on searching the Internet for a job and other career advice.

Finally, you will read about the best ways to evaluate a job offer and some important advice for on-the-job success. There is much to know in order to win in the job search game, but never fear! You have taken the first important step. After completing this book, you will have the knowledge, be able to apply the skills, and gain the strengths you need to ensure success at any stage of a career.

You are ready to begin a journey that will lead to a new position. The fun, the work, the achievements, the frustrations, the triumph: it all starts with a first step, your step. The journey to a new job is one with many steps and many experiences. But if you persevere, the payoff will be great. With your determination, the suggestions in this book, and a positive attitude in yourself and others, success *will* be yours.

JOB SEARCH STEPS

Now let's take a look at the chart below for the steps involved in a job search.

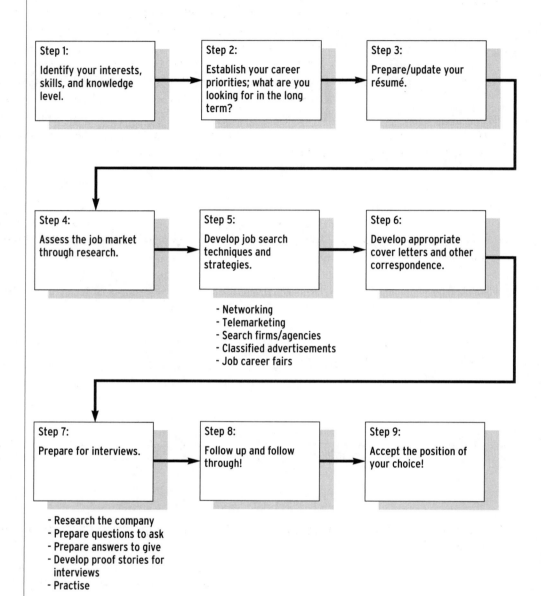

Step 1:

Identify your interests, skills, and knowledge level.

Step 2:

Establish your career priorities; what are you looking for in the long term?

Step 3:

Prepare/update your résumé.

Step 4:

Assess the job market through research.

Step 5:

Develop job search techniques and strategies.

Step 6:

Develop appropriate cover letters and other correspondence.

- Networking
- Telemarketing
- Search firms/agencies
- Classified advertisements
- Job career fairs

Step 7:

Prepare for interviews.

Step 8:

Follow up and follow through!

Step 9:

Accept the position of your choice!

- Research the company
- Prepare questions to ask
- Prepare answers to give
- Develop proof stories for interviews
- Practise

PRE-ASSESSMENT SURVEY

This survey is a tool to help you compare your thinking before and after you have completed this book. So grab a pencil and answer the following questions. If you don't have all the answers, that's OK! Just put a question mark down for now. These questions should feel a lot less foreign to you after you have focused more on them through discussions and exercises. Near the end of this book, there is a similar survey for you to complete. After completing the second survey, you will be able to compare the two surveys to see the development of your views of yourself and your job search strategies. You will later discover that you see things in much sharper focus!

1. How would you describe your ideal job? What type of activities or responsibilities would you like to have? In what type of business or industry do you see yourself working?

2. What are your personal traits or general job experiences that you would highlight as part of your job search strategy?

3. How do you intend to structure your résumé and what action verbs would be primary in describing your experiences and responsibilities?

4. How long should your résumé be, and how would you determine what to put in and what to leave out?

5. What are some of the best methods to research potential employers? What types of information would be useful to learn?

6. What is your personal strategy for marketing yourself to employers? What media would you use? How will you let employers know who you are and that you are available? Where will you go to look for positions?

7. What types of questions will you probably be asked during interviews? What types of questions should you ask during interviews?

8. What techniques will you use to market yourself during interviews?

9. Do you think you will have to take any tests as part of your career search? What types?

10. How will you stay motivated during your career search?

**CHAPTER
OBJECTIVES**

*After completing this
chapter, you will:*

*Determine your degree of
readiness to sell yourself.*

*Obtain a better understand-
ing and awareness of
yourself.*

*Identify your abilities, skills
and work values and
performances.*

2 KNOWING YOURSELF:

The Assessment Game

In order to be successful in any career search, it is imperative that you know yourself. Would a salesperson try to sell a product about which he or she knew little? Of course not. The same is true for a personal job search. First, you need to take some time to think carefully about yourself. The interesting thing about this part of your career planning is that many of us are too busy, or perhaps too uncertain, to be willing to enter into self-examination. This is a mistake. You must not skip this step in your process. If you do, your résumé will be weak, your research may be undirected, and your interviewing skills will be substandard. Is that any way to conduct a successful job search? Of course not. So let's sit back and take some time to examine some important things about ourselves and our lives.

In this chapter, you are presented with several tools to use in performing self-assessment. A word of caution is necessary: These tools will not tell you everything you may need to know to make basic career decisions. However, the insights gained from thinking about the issues raised in these few self-assessment exercises can help you establish a strong, knowledgeable approach to your career development.

Listed below are self-assessment tools described in this chapter that you are encouraged to complete.

- ■ Sales Readiness Quiz
- ■ Self-Awareness Checklist
- ■ Ability Assessment
- ■ Check Your Personality
- ■ Transferable Skills Checklist
- ■ Work Values and Preferences

A worksheet designed to help you summarize some of the things you have discovered about yourself is provided at the end of this chapter.

**SALES
READINESS QUIZ**

Do you have a "sales personality"? Are you "market-oriented" and "sales-minded"? According to the experts, those are the qualities you'll need to get the job of your choice. What follows is not a test of your knowledge of sales techniques: it is a quiz to evaluate your sales personality and your attitude toward selling in general by asking about your views about selling yourself in the job market. Be honest with yourself as you take this quiz. Go with your instincts, not with what you think the answer should be. You can't fail this quiz; it is only meant as a guide to help you judge your sales readiness.

Circle the responses that best describe you. Use the Quiz Rating Scale at the end of the quiz to determine your score. Then check the Sales Readiness Categories at the end of the quiz to determine how your score reflects your sales readiness.

1. You are planning a vacation with a friend. You want to go to Paris, and your friend wants to go on a cruise. Would you:
   A. Talk dynamically about Paris and what you love about it?
   B. Debate or ignore every reason he presents for going on the cruise?
   C. Try to find out what it is about the cruise that appeals to your friend most?

2. What is the most difficult aspect of getting a job?
   A. Finding the right job opportunities
   B. Asking for the job at the interview
   C. Calling to make the appointment

3. When you picture a salesperson in your mind's eye, do you see:
   A. A person who is trying to help you solve a problem?
   B. An arm-twisting used-car salesperson?
   C. A smooth persuader whose main motive is to sell a product or service?

4. Your main goal at a job interview is:
   A. To get the job
   B. To get as much information as possible
   C. To ask questions

5. When you solve a major problem at work, do you:
   A. Go in and ask for a raise?
   B. Write it down and bring it up at performance appraisal time?
   C. Give it little notice and assume your boss is keeping an eye on all your accomplishments?

6. You are planning to buy three pairs of expensive shoes in a small boutique. Do you:
   A. Pay for them?
   B. Ask at the beginning if they'll give a discount if you buy all three?
   C. After trying on shoes for three hours, say, "I might buy if you give a discount for buying three pairs"?

7. The last time someone said no to you, did you:
   A. Ask why he or she said no?
   B. Take the no as an irrevocable decision?
   C. Keep trying to persuade him or her to say yes?

8. In a group of very aggressive, talkative people, do you:
   A. Hold your own comfortably?
   B. Sit back timidly, content to listen?
   C. Speak up occasionally because you don't want to be left out?

9. If someone asked you to describe your best feature, would you:
   A. Talk nonstop for hours?
   B. Blush and not know where to start?
   C. Discuss briefly two or three admirable traits?

10. If you hear about a job opening, do you:
    A. Send a résumé?
    B. Call personnel to get more information?
    C. Try to contact the person you'd actually be working for?

11. How would you prepare for a job interview?
    A. Role-play with friends or colleagues
    B. Develop a list of questions to ask
    C. Think about what you'll be asked and prepare some answers

12. When sending out a letter with your résumé to a prospective employer, do you:
    A. Send a form letter?
    B. Think about not sending a letter?
    C. Write a tailored letter for each job?

13. If you call a prospective employer and he or she immediately says "We're not hiring today," what do you think is the reason?
    A. The employer took an instant dislike to you
    B. It's not the right time
    C. He or she doesn't have a good reason to talk to you

14. If you were selling computers and needed customers, would you:
    A. Call up all your friends?
    B. Attend a seminar on "Computer Basics for Small Business Owners?"
    C. Open a phone book and start calling?

15. You have applied for a job you really want and have been turned down by personnel. Would you:
    A. Call and try to get another appointment?
    B. Accept the decision and try another company?
    C. Try to find out whom you would be reporting to and make an appointment directly with that person?

16. Why do you think people "buy"?
    A. Because it makes them feel good
    B. Because their buying is based on a logical decision
    C. Because they like the salesperson

17. You are going on an important interview. Do you:
    A. Research the company?
    B. Wing it?
    C. Figure you'll ask questions to learn what you need to know at the interview?

18. A friend gives you a referral. Do you:
    A. Take the name and number and say, "I'll call next week"?
    B. Take the name and number and call immediately?
    C. Ask your friend for more information about the job and the boss?

19. Why is listening such an important part of the sales process?
    A. You get important information
    B. You find out the hidden concerns
    C. It shows that you care

20. What is the best way to stay in control during a sales presentation or a job interview?
    A. Always have a planned question
    B. Keep talking in a very persuasive manner
    C. Answer every objection or concern that is raised

21. At the end of a job interview, do you:
    A. Say thank you and leave?
    B. Ask for the job?
    C. Ask when you'll be hearing from the employer?

22. You've been searching for a job for six months and have been rejected twenty times. Do you:
    A. Get angry and take it out on friends and family?
    B. Begin to doubt your own abilities?
    C. Reevaluate your interviewing skills?

23. In an interview situation, which would you see as a strong signal of acceptance?
    A. If the interviewer asks, "When can you start?"
    B. If the interviewer says, "This would be your desk"
    C. If the interview goes on for a long time

24. You get a letter from a satisfied customer commending you, or a memo from a colleague complementing your performance. Do you:
    A. Show it to your family, friends, and colleagues?
    B. Acknowledge it, feel good, and stash it away?
    C. Make copies and send it to your boss, her boss, and even the president?

25. Who do you think gets to the top in most organizations?
    A. People who work the hardest
    B. People who fit into the corporate culture
    C. People who sell themselves most effectively

QUIZ RATING SCALE

Assign point values as indicated below to the responses you have given. Read the related discussions below the point values, and add up your total points.

1. A=3   B=1   C=5
The worst way to sell anything is to ignore or argue with the other person (B). You only hurt his feelings or make him want to cling stubbornly to his own position. Talking dynamically about Paris (A) may help, but the real secret to selling is to appeal to what the other person wants or needs. By finding out what's most appealing about the cruise (C), you'll know what the other person really wants. If he says, "There's a lot of dancing on board ship," for instance, you can counter with a list of places to go dancing in Paris.

2. A=3   B=5   C=3
Even the most experienced salespeople sometimes have difficulty "asking for the order" (B). When you're in an interview (the ultimate sales situation), an essential sales skill is knowing how to be assertive without being aggressive. Finding job opportunities (A) is not difficult if you take advantage of research tools available in the papers, the library, and personal contacts. Calling to make the appointment (C), also an important skill, is not difficult if you utilize the three Ps: patience, practice, and perseverance.

3. A=5   B=0   C=1

Your own notion of what a salesperson is will determine your ability to succeed in today's job market. If you see salespeople as arm twisters (B), you won't
feel very good about having to sell yourself. If you see a person who's trying to
help you solve your problems (A), that's the kind of salesperson you'll be during your job hunt. Smooth persuaders (C) will probably always do well in this
world. But they will probably always finish second to someone genuinely concerned with solving other people's problems.

4. A=5   B=5   C=5

All three of these answers are good. You want to come away with a job offer
so you can decide whether or not to take the job (A). You want to get as much
information as possible so you can make a smart decision about the job (B).
And you want to go in prepared to ask questions (C) in order to accomplish A
and B.

5. A=5   B=3   C=1

If you go right in and ask for a raise, you're sales oriented and interested in
building your value (A). This is the best approach, in step with today's more
assertive approach to life. Waiting for performance appraisal time is good (B),
but that may be a long time off. One philosophy is that it's more important to keep
yourself in the eye of the organization. You do this by letting people know when
you've done something valuable. If you give it little notice (C), no one else will
notice it either. If you don't sell yourself, nobody else will.

6. A=1   B=3   C=5

Negotiation is an important selling skill. The best time to ask for a discount is
after a salesperson has invested time showing her wares (C). At that point, she'd
rather give you a deal than lose the sale. You get three points for being able to
ask for a discount when you come in (B). You're on the right track, but you
don't want to tip your hand at the inning. You get one point (A) for being successful enough in the first place to be able to afford paying full price for three.

7. A=5   B=1   C=3

It's important to know why someone says no (A) if you want to get a yes the next
time. It might even tell you how to proceed to change the no to a yes this time.
If you keep trying to make the sale (C), you're not easily dissuaded and have
enough confidence in yourself to try again. If you take every no as an irrevocable
decision (B), you're not giving yourself a chance to learn what your mistake
might have been.

8. A=5   B=2   C=3

Congratulations on holding your own (A) and feeling comfortable about it.
Competition for jobs will be great, and the better your communications skills,
the easier you'll find it to sell yourself and the better your chances of getting the
jobs you want. Speaking up occasionally (C) gets you three points for realizing
that you need at least to make an effort to participate. You get two points for
listening (B) because you may gain valuable information. But you'll need to
learn to hold your own in a conversation if you're going to compete in the job
market.

9. A=1   B=3   C=5

Talking nonstop about your product (in this case, you) is not a very effective sales technique (A). Your customers will see you as pushy or unconcerned with their welfare. If you blush and don't know where to start (B), it means you're unprepared for the question. You wouldn't start selling cars without knowing anything about them. You'd prepare yourself for the questions your customers will most likely ask. If your answer was (C), it shows you think enough of yourself to discuss your good qualities without being obnoxious.

10. A=1   B=2   C=5

If you emulate successful salespeople, you'll take the initiative, be more assertive, and go directly to the person who makes the final hiring decision (C). Since you've heard about the position, use your source to get your foot in the door: "Johnny Jones suggested I call ...." Calling personnel to get more information (B) is less helpful but shows you're willing to do some research. If you just send a résumé to personnel (A), you're not taking advantage of your inside knowledge.

11. A=5   B=5   C=5

This is another question where all three answers are good. Doing well at job interviews takes skill, and the way to build a skill is to be well prepared and practise, practise, practise. So all three answers will be helpful to you.

12. A=2   B=0   C=5

Sending a résumé with no cover letter at all (B) tells a potential employer that you have no special interest in her or her company. The sales oriented approach is to let the employer know why she should read the résumé and call you in for an interview. You do this by sending a letter tailored specifically for her (C). Sending a form letter is almost as bad as no letter at all (A).

13. A=1   B=3   C=5

In selling terms, you've encountered *sales resistance in this situation,* which occasionally occurs when the customer doesn't like the salesperson (A). But in this case you hadn't been speaking long enough for the employer to dislike you (unless you were rude or obnoxious). It's possible that the employer was busy and you caught him at a bad time (B). But the most common reason for resistance is that the salesperson hasn't established the value of the product or service (C) in other words, hasn't presented a strong enough reason for the customer to buy (or for the employer to keep talking to you). If this happens often when you call, it means you need to change your approach.

14. A=4   B=5   C=1

Calling all your friends (A) is an excellent way to start because networking is one of the best ways to find buyers for your product. Attending a seminar for new business owners (B) shows you have strong sales sensibilities. People who would attend such a seminar are "qualified" buyers; they're definitely in the market for your product, so your chances of making a sale here are very good. Just opening the phone book (C) and making calls may bring you a few customers, but you'll probably waste most of your time and effort. In the job search, the more qualified buyers you reach, the better your chances of getting the job you want.

15. A=3   B=0   C=5

If you have been turned down by personnel and just accept their decision (B), you are too easily discouraged. Successful salespeople try to close the sale (get the person to buy) at least five times before they even consider giving up. Going directly to the decision maker (C) demonstrates sales smarts and persistence, both necessary and desirable qualities for the job search process. Trying to get another appointment through personnel (A) is not as effective but does show you're resilient and not easily put off.

16. A=5   B=1   C=3

Emotions play a big part in both selling and hiring processes. People buy (or hire) for emotional reasons (A); the product fulfills a need or desire they have. That's why, in order to sell yourself to an employer, you'll have to show him how you'll solve his problems or fulfill his needs. People also buy from people they like, trust, and respect (C). You can't make someone like you, but you can show that you are a person worthy of trust and respect. Logic almost always plays a lesser role in the decision-making process (B).

17. A=5   B=0   C=3

Although asking questions (C) is an essential part of the interviewing process, most people are impressed by what you *already* know about them. Before you go on any "sales call," learn as much as you can about the company and the person you're going to see (A). You'll stand out from other applicants. If you try to wing it (B), you put yourself at a definite disadvantage — you'll know nothing about the company or the job before sitting down with the interviewer.

18. A=1   B=3   C=5

The best answer in this case is to ask your friend for as much information as you can get before you make the call (C). You want to find out something about the person you'll be calling (who he or she is, what his or her position is in the company, etc.), what the job is like, and why this job is open. Calling immediately (B) shows you have initiative, but you'd be better off researching the company first. If you say "I'll call next week" (A), you're probably just putting it off and may lose the opportunity.

19. A=5   B=5   C=5

All three answers are true. There's an old saying that goes, "Customers don't care how much you know until they know how much you care." In a hiring situation, the interviewer wants to know how much you care about the job and the company (C). Listening carefully also gives you important factual information (A) and may reveal the hidden concerns of the individual interviewer (B), the real reasons you will or won't get hired.

20. A=5   B=1   C=3

Here is another sales maxim: "The person who asks the question controls the conversation." Going into the interview with a series of planned questions (A) keeps you in control of the situation and makes sure you get all the information you need to make a smart decision. What you think is talking in a persuasive manner (B) may come across as conceited and pushy. Without asking questions, you could end up talking for hours and never satisfy the employer's real concerns.

Clearly answering objections or concerns (C) is essential to a successful interview but doesn't give you the same control that asking questions does.

21. A=1   B=5   C=3

It's important that you "ask for the sale" or, in this case, the job (B). Ask in a pleasant, civil way so that you don't turn people off. Saying thank you and leaving (A) is not going to help you get the job unless you're the most sought-after person in the world. Asking when you'll be hearing from the employer (C) shows a little more assertiveness and is better than just saying thanks and leaving. But more than likely you'll be told. "We have several candidates to choose from. We'll call you."

22. A=0   B=1   C=5

The best answer here is to reevaluate your interviewing skills (C). Twenty interviews can give you a lot of good experience in different types of situations that may arise. Go over your experiences and ask yourself what you did right and what can be improved. If you begin to doubt your own abilities (B), you're taking rejection too personally. A negative decision may have nothing to do with your personality. Getting angry at yourself or at anyone else (A) doesn't improve your skills or your chances at the next interview. Don't give up trying; the next interview could be the one you've been waiting for!

23. A=3   B=5   C=1

Most people take a long interview as a sign of definite interest (C). In fact, this often signifies nothing more than a disorganized interviewer, someone who doesn't really know what he's looking for. Don't assume an hour-long interview means you're a shoe-in. If, however, the interviewer starts to visualize you in the job and consistently refers to "your" desk, "your" coworkers, etc. (B), it's a pretty good clue that there is a strong interest. "When can you start?" (A) is a possible sign of interest, but it may also indicate that the employer is in urgent need of someone and may not be able to wait until you're available.

24. A=3   B=1   C=5

Are you secure enough to take hold of your future and make sure the right people see what others think of you? Since only the rich and famous have public relations agents, we have to assume that role for ourselves. The best answer is (C). Showing the letter to your friends and colleagues (A) will make you feel better and perhaps add to your reputation but may not do much where your boss is concerned. Feeling good is always nice (B), but why pass up opportunities to increase your visibility?

25. A=3   B=4   C=5

Although we're in the middle of the information age, we're also at the beginning of the age of marketing. Even our prime ministers have to "sell" themselves if they want to get elected. You must be well versed in sales and marketing skills to get ahead (C). Corporate fit is and will continue to be important (B) but work is becoming less structured in many situations. Hard workers (A) are not to be discounted but they are not necessarily the people who get ahead. In a small or newly organized company this may be the case, but unless other people know how hard you work, or unless you "fit in" with the rest of the team, your hard work will not always be appreciated.

SALES READINESS CATEGORIES

96 - 120 points

Good for you! You've scored high in sales readiness which means you're one step ahead of the competition already. You have a positive attitude toward selling and a personality that makes you a natural for marketing yourself!

71 - 95 points

You are well on your way toward the sales and marketing orientation required for success in today's market. You're thinking in the right direction, and with just a little improvement, there'll be no stopping you!

46 - 70 points

You're not quite at the level you should be, but you're getting there. It would help you to be a bit more assertive and to have more confidence in yourself. All it takes is a shift in attitude and a willingness learn. You're on the right track.

45 points or less

You need to reevaluate your attitudes and perceptions regarding sales and marketing. Doing the exercises and following the advice in this book will be a great help in improving your readiness to market yourself and increasing your job search know-how.

How well did you score as a salesperson? What did you learn about yourself? Are there any aspects of selling yourself that need improvement? Write your thoughts below, focusing on ways to strengthen your sales readiness.

_____

_____

_____

_____

_____

_____

_____

_____

_____

_____

_____

_____

_____

_____

SELF-AWARENESS CHECKLIST

An important part of self-assessment for your job search should focus on self-awareness. How aware are you of the ways you perceive yourself and others? How much do you know about the ways you react to situations? To determine your own level of self-awareness, read the statements below and place a check mark in the boxes that correspond to how much or how often you feel this way. Use this page to help you think about how you perceive yourself and how you wish to be perceived.

	Always	Often	Sometimes	Rarely	Never
I am eager to learn.	❑	❑	❑	❑	❑
My work is exciting.	❑	❑	❑	❑	❑
I'm willing to listen with an open mind.	❑	❑	❑	❑	❑
I constantly have new insights.	❑	❑	❑	❑	❑
I like taking direction from people who know something I don't.	❑	❑	❑	❑	❑
I try to look at the world through the eyes of the other person.	❑	❑	❑	❑	❑
When someone is talking to me, I really listen.	❑	❑	❑	❑	❑
I'm honest with myself and others.	❑	❑	❑	❑	❑
I've thought about my own strengths and weaknesses.	❑	❑	❑	❑	❑
I'm sensitive to others' needs.	❑	❑	❑	❑	❑
I care for and am concerned about others.	❑	❑	❑	❑	❑
I adapt easily to the environment and situation.	❑	❑	❑	❑	❑
I am willing to take risks.	❑	❑	❑	❑	❑
I am satisfied with the way I look physically.	❑	❑	❑	❑	❑
I am satisfied with the way I feel physically.	❑	❑	❑	❑	❑

ABILITY ASSESSMENT

In our day-to-day lives, we don't often take time to take serious assessment of ourselves. This is critical to conducting a successful job search. In this instrument, we will take a look at what you consider to be your talents and examine a variety of areas of ability in an attempt to pinpoint your unique qualities.

Ability categories are defined on the following pages. Evaluate yourself on each of these according to the following scale:

1	=	No ability at all
2	=	Enough ability to get by with some help
3	=	Some natural ability
4	=	Definite, strong ability
5	=	Outstanding ability

When evaluating the following, try not to compare yourself with any particular reference group such as other students, other colleagues, the general population, etc. Just focus on rating yourself according to your best assessment of your individual capability.

Verbal/Persuasive

Writing: express self well in writing

Talking: express self well in ordinary conversation

Speaking: able to deliver a speech, address an audience

Persuading: able to convince others of your view

Selling: able to convince others to purchase a product or service

Negotiating: able to bargain or assist in the bargaining process

Social

Social ease: can relax and enjoy social situations such as parties or receptions

Appearance: able to dress appropriately and presentably for a variety of interpersonal or group occasions

Self-esteem: able to maintain a positive view of self, including accepting negative feedback or criticism

Dealing with public: can continually relate to a broad cross-section of people who need information, service, or help

Technical

Computational speed: able to manipulate numerical data rapidly and accurately without using any mechanical device

Working with data: able to comfortably work with large amounts of data

Comprehension: ability to compile, interpret and present such data

Computer use: able to use electronic computers to solve problems, knowledge of programming, and familiarity with various computer capabilities

Investigative

_____ Scientific curiosity: comfortable with scientific method of inquiry, knowledge of scientific phenomena

_____ Research: ability to gather information in a systematic way for a certain field of knowledge

Creative

_____ Artistic: sensitivity to aesthetics, able to create works of art

_____ Use of imagination: able to create new ideas, forms with various physical objects

_____ Use of imagination: able to create new ideas by merging abstract ideas in new ways

Working with Others

_____ Supervisory: able to oversee, direct, and manage work of others

_____ Teaching: able to help others learn how to do something or to understand something, provide insight

_____ Coaching: able to instruct or train for improvement of performance

_____ Counselling: able to develop helping relationship with another individual

Managerial

_____ Organization and planning: able to develop a program, project, or set of ideas with systematic preparation and arrangement of tasks. Can coordinate people and resources as well

_____ Orderliness: Able to arrange items in a regular fashion so that information can be readily retrieved and used

_____ Handling details: able to work with a variety or volume of information without losing track

_____ Making decisions: able to comfortably make judgments or reach conclusions about matters which require action: able to accept responsibility for consequences of such actions

Now that you have reviewed the lists above and reflected on your own variety of abilities, decide which you believe represent your most prominent strengths. Refer to those areas that have fours and fives. Now choose which are your most outstanding and noteworthy abilities. List them below. Remember these as you continue to focus on the personal abilities and skills you have to offer an employer.

_____

_____

_____

_____

CHECK YOUR PERSONALITY

The following several pages will help assess your personal traits and skills. This type of self-knowledge is critical not only to your understanding and appreciation of yourself, but also for the later development of your résumé and interviewing skills. Read through the following traits and check any that you feel identify characteristics you presently possess. Keep a list of your most prominent traits to be used later to showcase yourself during interviews.

___ Accurate	___ Decisive	___ Loving	___ Self-controlled
___ Active	___ Dignified	___ Mature	___ Sensitive
___ Adaptable	___ Dominant	___ Methodical	___ Serious
___ Adventurous	___ Easygoing	___ Modest	___ Sociable
___ Aggressive	___ Energetic	___ Motivated	___ Strong-minded
___ Alert	___ Enthusiastic	___ Open-minded	___ Strong-willed
___ Ambitious	___ Extroverted	___ Optimistic	___ Supportive
___ Analytical	___ Flexible	___ Organized	___ Teachable
___ Assertive	___ Forceful	___ Original	___ Tenacious
___ Broad-minded	___ Forgiving	___ Outgoing	___ Tolerant
___ Calm	___ Frank	___ Patient	___ Understanding
___ Capable	___ Generous	___ Persevering	___ Uninhibited
___ Cautious	___ Helpful	___ Poised	___ Verbal
___ Cheerful	___ Honest	___ Practical	___ Versatile
___ Clear-thinking	___ Humorous	___ Purposeful	___ Warm
___ Competitive	___ Independent	___ Rational	___ Wise
___ Confident	___ Industrious	___ Realistic	___ Witty
___ Considerate	___ Intelligent	___ Reliable	
___ Cooperative	___ Inventive	___ Resourceful	
___ Curious	___ Logical	___ Self-confident	
___ Creative	___ Likeable	___ Responsible	

TRANSFERABLE SKILLS CHECKLIST

Transferable skills are those skills that you have developed from previous jobs, volunteer work, life experiences, or any other arena where you have developed some general competencies. These competencies can be very valuable in marketing yourself to employers — especially if you are a recent college graduate with little direct business or industry experience. These skills, gained in other settings, can be transferred into the new position you seek. Review the list of transferable skills below and check the ones that you feel you have. Keep these transferable skills in mind. We will be using a similar checklist when we discuss résumé preparation. Use these two checklists to help you write a résumé that will promote your worth to a potential employer.

___ advise people
___ analyze data
___ anticipate problems
___ arrange functions
___ assemble products/build
___ audit records
___ budget money
___ buy products/services
___ calculate/manipulate numbers
___ check for accuracy
___ collect money
___ communicate
___ consult with others
___ coordinate activities
___ cope with deadlines
___ correspond
___ create
___ delegate
___ demonstrate
___ design
___ develop
___ direct others
___ do precision work
___ do public relations
___ drive
___ edit
___ encourage
___ endure long hours
___ enforce
___ evaluate
___ examine
___ file records

___ find information
___ follow directions
___ follow through
___ handle complaints
___ handle equipment
___ handle money
___ help people
___ implement
___ improve
___ install
___ interpret data
___ interview people
___ investigate
___ lead people
___ learn quickly
___ listen
___ make policy
___ manage a business
___ manage people
___ mediate problems
___ meet the public
___ memorize information
___ mentor others
___ negotiate
___ nurture
___ observe
___ perceive needs
___ persuade others
___ plan
___ program
___ protect property
___ raise money

WORK VALUES AND LIFE PREFERENCES

When making a career decision, it is important to look at values and life preferences. When you identify areas that are important to you, this can help guide you to a position with which you will be satisfied.

The following inventory lists work values and life preferences. Reflect on what is really important to you in these areas and indicate your preferences. Place an X on the line that reflects the degree of importance for that item. If you strongly prefer to be self-employed, you would place your mark for question one under the 2 on the left below. If you are neutral about whether you work alone or with people, you would place your mark for question two under the zero (0) below. If you have a strong preference for a structured environment, you would place your mark for question three under the 2 on the right below.

	2	**1**	**0**	**1**	**2**	
1. Self-employed	__	__	__	__	__	Work in a company
2. Work with others	__	__	__	__	__	Work alone
3. Creative environment	__	__	__	__	__	Structured environment
4. No supervision	__	__	__	__	__	Close supervision
5. Extended work hours	__	__	__	__	__	Standard 8-hour day
6. Similar duties daily	__	__	__	__	__	Variety of duties
7. Possible overtime	__	__	__	__	__	Guaranteed regular hours
8. Security	__	__	__	__	__	Challenge, risk
9. Slow pace, little pressure	__	__	__	__	__	Fact pace, high pressure
10. Little, no travel	__	__	__	__	__	Frequent travel
11. Small business	__	__	__	__	__	Large business
12. Live in rural area	__	__	__	__	__	Live in urban area
13. Live alone	__	__	__	__	__	Live with people
14. Desire culture and community	__	__	__	__	__	Little need for culture and community
15. Spend money	__	__	__	__	__	Save money

After you have worked through the items above, answer these questions as specifically as you can.

1. What work values and life preferences are most important to you?

_____

_____

_____

_____

_____

_____

_____

_____

2. In what ways might these work values and life preferences affect your career decision making?

_____

_____

_____

_____

_____

_____

_____

_____

QUESTIONS

1. Why is it important to do self-assessment before beginning a job search?

1. What was your score on the Sales Readiness Quiz? Based on this sales ability score, will you have to make adjustments in the way you approach marketing yourself for a job?

2. Using the lists found on pp. 17 and 18, what are the top three personality traits and transferable skills you possess? How will you be able to showcase these traits on your résumé and during the interview?

CHAPTER
OBJECTIVES

*After completing this
chapter, you will:*

*Identify various types of
résumés and determine
which is best for you.*

*Create a detailed, dynamic
résumé that is inviting and
easy to read.*

*Understand the dynamics of
and create a scannable
résumé.*

*Identify selected Internet
sites on résumé writing and
posting.*

3 THE RÉSUMÉ:

Your Ticket to Interviews

Developing the résumé is an important part of your job search and is usually one of the first steps taken in the job search process. Preparing your résumé is something you will want to do several times in the course of your career since it needs to be updated to reflect any changes in your professional life and to include any new skills you have developed.

A résumé cannot get you a job; however, a good résumé can help you get to the interview stage. And an interview is a requirement before a job offer is made. So, résumé writing is serious business, and something that requires considerable effort. This chapter includes the following discussions to assist you in your résumé preparation:

- Types of résumés
- Guidelines, sections, tips
- Computer-generated résumé
- Electronic résumé
- Education/experience worksheets
- Sample résumés
- Résumé checklist
- Internet résumé sites

TYPES OF RÉSUMÉS

There are three ways you can structure your résumé: reverse chronological, functional, and combination. Some recruiters have indicated that they like the more recent format of the combination résumé, but the choice is up to you.

In the **reverse chronological résumé** format, information is organized according to time. The most recent education and experience are listed first working back to the earlier education and experience. This is by far the most widely-used type of résumé because of its simplicity. This is an appropriate format to use if you have had continual employment and are more interested in providing a rather historical view of your past. This résumé type is often most suitable for students and recent graduates.

In the **functional résumé** format, information is organized according to types of experiences or functions you have performed. Rather than relying on dates and time frames as in the reverse chronological format, this format spotlights key traits or qualities and provides details and cites examples of the demonstration of those qualities. This type of résumé requires a lot more thought and planning than the first; however, one of its strengths is that it is not like the majority of résumés that are written. This format is useful if you do not have continual employment experience and/or you are interested in focusing the attention of the reader on what you did rather than when and where you did it.

The **combination résumé** format is a fairly recent development. Here the benefits of both the reverse chronological and the functional formats are combined. Normally, this format begins with a type of personal summary or summation of key traits and skills. This summary is followed by the more traditional listing of information as in the chronological variety. This not only presents your key qualities in a brief promotional statement at the beginning, but it also gives the reader the more familiar structure of the chronological style.

RÉSUMÉ GUIDELINES

The résumé is a sales tool, and you are the salesperson who needs to use this tool effectively. Therefore, it is very important for you to pay attention to the appearance of your materials, as well as to the content. The way you put résumé information on the page should be as impressive and interesting in the way it appears as in the way it is worded. An impressive résumé is a blend of good content and attractive format.

Your résumé should read well and fast. You might not have more than five or ten seconds to attract the attention of the employer and encourage that person to read in more detail. Keep in mind that most of us read from the top of the page at the left margin down in a sort of fan direction when we are trying to scan a document to get the greatest amount of information in the least amount of time. This is also the way résumés are read because recruiters receive hundreds of résumés each day. It is important for your best and most important information to be close to the top of the page and for your format to be inviting and easy to read.

How long should your résumé be? The most common rule of thumb is one to two pages, particularly if you are a recent graduate. Remember: A résumé is not designed to be a complete personal history. It is more like a specification sheet about a product (you) written in such a way that the recruiter will want to learn more from you in person (the interview). At the same time, don't be preoccupied with squeezing your information onto one page. If you need more space for relevant information, take it. It is not recommended to include attachments to your résumé, such as grade transcripts, or letters of recommendation. This is extra information that may not be read at this preliminary step of the job search process. Remember how many résumés recruiters receive daily!

General writing style for a résumé is quite different from a letter or a business report. Instead of using complete sentences and lengthy paragraphs, your goal in presenting information résumé-style is quite the opposite. Use sentence fragments that express complete ideas. Start new ideas or phrases on the left-hand side of the page whenever possible, and use bullets or dashes to make the lines of type easier to read quickly. You should never use the word "I" on your résumé.

Your résumé needs to be accurate. Don't estimate or approximate anything, and make sure you are accurate throughout. Proofread it meticulously for relevant and clearly presented information. Two techniques for proofing are reading backwards and reading out loud. Read each word of your résumé starting at the end of the last line and working your way to the left and to the top. This can help you uncover misspellings and typos. Reading your résumé out loud can help ensure readability and completeness. Also examine it for any mechanical errors. Remember the positive impression you must make with this document, and do not have **any** misspellings or other grammatical errors.

RÉSUMÉ SECTIONS

Most résumés contain three basic sections: heading, education, and experience. Other special sections that can be included are career objective, qualification or skills, and personal sections. Following are brief descriptions of these sections.

Heading

Name, address, current, and/or permanent addresses. If possible, include both home and work numbers. Always remember to use postal codes. Many job seekers also include their e-mail addresses. This is a good practice and signals to the reader that you are using today's communication technology. Make sure if you include your e-mail address that you check it daily and that your address is appropriate.

If you have a personal home page, don't list it automatically in the heading of your résumé. Consider if you want it to be seen by a potential employer. Home page references on résumés are particularly appropriate for individuals desiring positions as Webmasters or Web designers. But remember: Any Web page referenced in a résumé should be professional looking and in good taste.

Education

How detailed you choose to be in this section depends on how long it has been since you were in school. Recent graduates will want to include grade point average, honours, campus activities. If you have been in the workforce for some time, you may merely wish to include your degree, school, and dates of study or year of graduation. For those who have been in the workforce for some time, showing education on the résumé may not be necessary.

Qualifications

This section has become a very important and useful section on the résumé. It should hold a prominent position in the résumé, even before your experience. In this section you can highlight the important skills, certificates, and training that are relevant to employment. Computer skills, languages, special licenses and certificates should all be included here.

Work Experience

Provide job titles, company names, and cities and provinces in which the companies are located. No need to include street addresses or names of managers or other personnel. Briefly describe the duties and responsibilities of each position. Use active verbs to show power and accomplishment. How far back should you go to list employment? That depends. The rule of thumb is five years; however, if you had some noteworthy experience previous to that time, you may wish to include it. Also, if you have worked for many years, you may want to include a greater number of work experiences.

Later in this chapter, you have two worksheets to assist you in effectively developing your ideas for the education and work experience.

Adding Impact to Your Work Experience

A useful technique to consider in creating a work experience section with more impact is to include more in your job descriptions than simple duties. Most résumé writers do a very good job of listing the job responsibilities that they have. The problem is that in most cases, you are telling the reader what he or she already knows: Sales people deal with customers and handle accounts, secretaries create documents and handle scheduling appointments, computer programmers program computers! See what we mean?

Try thinking about your work experience a little differently. As you reflect on your duties, also think about the scope of responsibilities you have had and your accomplishments on the job. Here are two examples using the positions of computer programmer and sales representative.

Computer Programmer position

Duty statement: Wrote code and performed troubleshooting using C language.

Scope statement: Worked as a member of a four-person project team to create code and solve programming problems in a PC-based environment.

Achievement statement:	Was responsible for writing and maintaining a C-based computer program which analyzed current work flow operations, reduced analysis time by 50 percent and served as a model program for six division offices.

Sales Representative position

Duty statement:	In charge of outside sales for computer division.
Scope statement:	In charge of selling electronic components to 140 clients in a three-province region of Canada.
Achievement statement:	Maintain successful three-province sales region of 140 clients averaging five new accounts monthly and generating a 30 percent increase in revenues over a six-month period.

See how this attention to scope and achievement in your job description is more powerful and certainly more informative? Which person would you rather talk to, the sales person who declared on his or her résumé that he or she was in charge of outside sales or the person who said that he or she is responsible for a 30 percent increase in revenues over a six-month period? I think you get the idea. By the way, don't despair if you don't have hugely impressive achievements at this stage in your life. That's OK. Just think about all aspects of past and present employment, and figure out how you can make the job experience section of your résumé move beyond the mundane description of job duties. Try to provide scope statements of your work, if not full-blown achievements. Remember, the résumé is one of your most important sales tools. Maximize its impact on the reader.

Career Objective

An objective is a clear and concise statement of the type of job you are seeking and the benefits the company will gain by hiring you. Be original, and avoid phrases such as "wish to gain experience" or "desire for advancement." You need to stress how you can benefit the company, not how the company can benefit you. Experts disagree on the usefulness of this section of the résumé. Some recruiters like to see a statement of career focus, while others just want to read the details that follow. A rule of thumb that could be followed is to include a career objective if you are a recent graduate or are changing fields or emphasis in your future work. If your previous experience demonstrates an established career area in which you wish to continue, an objective may not be necessary. Also, you may want to omit any specific career objective from your résumé and include it in your cover letter instead.

Personal/Professional Summary

Another option you have to a career objective is the personal or professional summary. This section has become a popular replacement for the career objective, is often easier to write, and may say more about you to the employer than a typical career objective statement. Instead of indicating the type of position desired, this section focuses on what you have accomplished and what technical or personal traits you have to offer. A reflection on the scopes of your positions and your accomplishments is very useful in creating a personal or professional summary. Many résumé writing software packages have built-in formats for these types of summary. Being able to produce a succinct yet specific paragraph or so about yourself and your qualifications can be impressive to most résumé readers, who tend pay closer attention to the material at the beginning of the résumé.

Personal

This is another section that experts don't always agree on. If you have the space, you may want to include a line or two about some personal characteristics or activities. Sometimes these comments help to make the person behind the résumé seem more real. At the same time, you must be careful not to mention anything in this section that could be controversial (political, religious views, etc.).

When you put these sections together to form your résumé, you need to remember that the most important information must go first. Therefore, if you are experienced, your work section will follow the heading. If you are a recent graduate, education will be your most prominent section. Your qualifications should always be near the top. In any event, if you include a personal section, it should be placed near or at the end of the résumé. Last, your references should be supplied on a separate page. Some choose to make a statement that references will be supplied upon request. Employers will expect you to furnish references regardless.

RÉSUMÉ TIPS

Concerning the content of your résumé: Stay away from mentioning anything personal that is not directly related to the job. This includes your age or date of birth, your health, or even your social insurance number.

While many sources recommend that your résumé should only be one page this is often not realistic. Your main focus here is to attract the attention of the potential employer with your résumé. If your resume is too crowded on one page nothing will stand out. Do not be afraid to go to the second page but make sure that the most relevant information is on the first page. If you do use two pages make sure you put a header at the top with your name and phone number on the second page. This is useful if faxing your résumé. Imagine if only the second page is received. Without this phone number it is often impossible to track you down.

Electronic Delivery

The delivery method of résumés has changed dramatically in the last several years. Previously, most résumés were sent using Canada Post. Now, just as many employers are requesting that résumés be faxed to them as mailed to them. And some individuals are sending their résumés via electronic mail using their computers and modems. These new modes of delivery have affected how we create our résumés and even what type and colour of paper to use. *(Refer to the Electronic Résumés section on page 28 for further details.)*

Paper Choices

If you plan to send résumés by regular mail, the safe choice for paper colour is white or off-white. A beige, buff, or light grey colour can also be used. Avoid bright and unusual colours; the business community is still fairly conservative in nature. Résumés should be printed on good bond paper (at least 20 lb.). When using special shades or types of paper, corresponding blank sheets of paper (for cover letters and other correspondence) and full-sized envelopes should be purchased for a total, professional look. Special résumé paper and envelopes can be found in many office supply stores. If you plan to send a number of résumés via fax machine, quality of paper is not so important. Always remember that you should select a type style and print size that are easy to read.

Photos

Photographs are generally not recommended on résumés. For most people, photos are not relevant to the position they seek. However, there has been a growing trend to include photos on résumés which are displayed on the Internet. In these cases, photos should be used that can be downloaded quickly, and that lend to overall visual appeal. The use of photographs is a purely personal decision; however, the photo should not distract from the résumé itself.

Once you have finished a draft of your résumé, let it cool. Go back to it a few days later and read it with a critical eye. Then show it once again to a person or two whose opinions you value. Make any changes that would improve the document at this point. Remember, résumé writing is very subjective. Everyone seems to have an opinion, but there is no one right way to do it. Sometimes it is useful to seek out the opinions of others; however, if you receive too much conflicting advice, it is easy to become confused. Remember, this is *your* document. You need to be satisfied with it.

COMPUTER GENERATED RÉSUMÉS

Today the computer is helping to make many routine tasks easier and less tedious. Résumé writing is one of these tasks. There are many books with disks and software programs on the market to aid in the writing and formatting of résumés. You are encouraged to look into these programs as an alternative to typing everything from scratch yourself. Some programs will allow a full range of choices in both format and content. Others will prompt you with questions to determine information. Still others will use one standard format. Regardless of these choices, however, you still will need to think about what you want to say and how you want to write it. You are still the creator of this piece.

ELECTRONIC RÉSUMÉS

New technology has reshaped the future of the employment process in ways that were never even dreamed of just a decade ago. Computers have changed the rules of the job search game. To understand this phenomenon and use it to your advantage, you need to examine just what an electronic résumé is, how it differs from traditional résumés, and the implications that all this has for you as you begin the job search.

What Are Electronic Résumés ?

The term **electronic résumé** can be used to describe résumés that will be scanned by computer and résumés that are placed on the Internet for reading. Both are electronic, and both differ greatly from the traditional, paper résumé. Résumés that are scanned into software programs by employers are very focused, basic, and rely on key points or traits to promote individuals. Résumés placed on the Internet for reading tend to look like traditional résumés at the beginning, but the reader may soon discover that he or she can travel to many other sites, hyper-texted in the electronic résumé, for further information, materials, and sometimes even multimedia presentations.

Let's look further at the scannable variety of electronic résumé. To understand what is needed in a scannable résumé, let's first examine the capabilities of this new résumé scanning technology.

Résumé scanning software, which is being used fairly extensively by Fortune 500 companies and is becoming popular in other firms, can perform many functions such as résumé scanning, tracking résumés in the system, and generating response letters to applicants. Some systems help firms keep track of who has been hired and information relating to their job applications. Most systems perform the same way. Three of the most common are Resumix, Restrac, and SmartSearch2.

How Do They Work?

This is how a résumé program works. As hard copy or paper résumés are scanned into computers, the program looks for key words identified by company personnel as important. For example, a department manager may have the database search for a candidate with these traits:

4 years teleconference training, JIT (Just-In-Time) Inventory Control

In addition to the types of information listed above, some programs can identify desirable employment traits and place them in various categories such as "must have," "important to have," "nice to have," or "must not have." Résumé software programs can rank résumés according to the number of "hits" or "matches" between the key words identified and those appearing on the résumé.

Why Do Companies Use Résumé-Scanning Programs?

Most companies use these programs because they save time and energy. A computer can scan and store a résumé in seconds and can quickly retrieve it a year later if necessary. Scanning programs can objectively review information on résumés. Companies feel the systems enable them to respond more quickly to applicants than in the past. Also, candidates who inquire about the status of their résumés can be given information quickly. Companies do not use these programs because they are inexpensive, however. Some can cost as much as $500 000. However, if they can make the recruitment process run smoother and more efficiently in mid- to large-sized companies, it can be well worth the cost.

Tips For Working With the Electronic Recruitment Process

To help you make the determination of which type of résumé is appropriate with which company, first call the company whenever possible to see if it uses computer scanning software. Find out if the company has an Internet job site to further aid you in your application process. No matter how you transmit your résumé initially, remember to take an attractive, more traditional copy of it to the interview.

Résumé Scanning Tips

Here is some advice to keep in mind when preparing a résumé to be scanned.

- Use plain white paper measuring 81/2 x 11 inches.
- Use standard 10 to 14-point font.
- Use keyword summary and industry jargon.
- Don't feel you must limit the résumé to one page.
- Don't use **bold**, *italic,* or underlining.
- Don't use shading, boxes, or borders.
- Don't staple or fold the résumé.

To ensure that your résumé scans well, you should avoid most of the graphical techniques used in conventional résumés to catch the attention of human viewers. The scanner works best with simplicity.

Avoid the following when creating a scannable résumé:

Technique to Avoid	Reason
Italics, underlining, fancy typefaces	Scanners need clear, distinct characters or they will "see" blots and blurs rather than letters.
Columns or any other kind of landscaping	Scanners read from left to right, so columns look like different pages on the same page to a scanner; diagrams and pictures can confuse scanners because these devices are designed primarily to read text.

| Shading | Scanners need clear contrast between letters and background, so shading increases the likelihood of errors by a scanner. |
| Boxes | Scanners are confused by the vertical lines in boxes, which they may read as the letter "I." |

(Keep in mind that sources may vary on this advice. There are no agreed-upon rules at this point.)

Advice on Using Scannable Résumés

The electronic era has ushered in new considerations and techniques for those wishing to compete for positions in the new millennium. Gone are the days when one could just stuff a résumé into an envelope and turn it over to the mail. Applicants now must contact companies to see if résumé scanning software is used.

If companies are using this new technology, avoid sending several résumés to the same company. Once your résumé is scanned, it is in that firm's permanent file. Faxing résumés is not recommended if the scanning software is used. When following up to determine the disposition of your résumé, consider using these questions "Did you receive my résumé?" "Was I a match in your desired skill areas?" "How has my résumé been routed?"

Some experts feel the operative word for finding out if your résumé (and you) have made it to the next step of the screening process is "routed." If you follow some of the advice and recommendations above and if you can demonstrate you are a good candidate for a position, you stand a good chance of being routed or in the loop and on your way to the interview.

WORKSHEETS FOR EDUCATION AND WORK EXPERIENCE

Because you are the one who has to take your educational activities and work experiences and discuss them in a concise yet interesting way for your résumé, here are some tools to help. Most individuals find it easy to calculate the time they have worked at a company or the degrees or training they have received; however, it is not always that easy to display these experiences in an attractive and dynamic way. The following can provide a little practise in talking about your education and work experiences on paper. After you have completed the worksheets, you can use the information and experiences in writing to generate the actual wording for your résumé.

ACTION VERBS FOR EDUCATION AND EXPERIENCE SECTIONS

To ensure a dynamic and powerful résumé, you will want to begin your discussions of school and work experiences and responsibilities with action verbs. Read through the following list circling the verbs that can be applied to you in your school and/or work activities. Keep this page in front of you as you draft your résumé sections.

Act/perform	Coordinate	Find	Learn	Process	Service
Adapt	Cope	Fix	Listen	Produce	Set
Advise	Create	Gather	Locate	Program	Solve
Analyze	Decide	Generate	Log	Promote	Sort
Anticipate	Delegate	Handle complaints	Maintain	Protect	Speak
Appraise	Deliver	Handle equipment	Manage	Question	Study
Arrange	Demonstrate	Handle money	Mediate	Raise	Supervise
Assemble	Design	Help people	Meet public	Read	Support
Assess	Determine	Illustrate	Memorize	Reduce	Test
Audit	Develop	Implement	Mentor	Recommend	Teach
Budget	Direct	Improve	Motivate	Report	Train
Calculate	Distribute	Inform	Negotiate	Research	Translate
Check	Enforce	Initiate	Observe	Resolve	Troubleshoot
Collect	Entertain	Inspect	Obtain	Restore	Update
Communicate	Estimate	Install	Operate	Retrieve	Understand
Compare	Evaluate	Instruct	Order	Review	Upgrade
Compile	Examine	Interpret	Organize	Run	Verify
Compute	Exhibit	Interview	Perform	Schedule	Volunteer
Confront	Expand	Invent	Persuade	Select	Work
Contact	Explain	Investigate	Plan	Sell	Write
Control	Explore	Lead	Prepare		

REPRESENTING EDUCATION ACTIVITY

This exercise is designed to help you think about aspects of your education. By answering the following questions, you will be constructing, piece by piece, the educational section of your résumé.

1. State the name of the educational institution you most recently attended. Include the city and province in which the school is located.

   _____

   _____

2. Write the correct name of the diploma/degree you are working to attain or have attained.

   _____

3. Supply the month and year of your graduation. _____

4. Indicate your grade point average (for recent graduates). _____

5. List any honours or academic achievements.

   _____

   _____

6. List several of your favourite courses or classes in which you did well.

   _____

   _____

7. List courses involving subject matter that relates to the career you are pursuing.

   _____

   _____

   _____

8. Decide what coursework you would like to mention in your résumé. Consider grouping courses into several categories with appropriate headings.

   _____

9. Highlight any special equipment (computers or other types) and any software or computer languages that you have either learned in school or taught yourself.

_____

_____

_____

_____

10. List any other post-secondary school educational institutions attended. Give names and locations.

_____

11. If you obtained a diploma/degree from the institution above indicate the title below, along with the date of graduation.

_____

12. List any honours or special comments about coursework for the above educational experience.

_____

13. If your high school graduation was within the past several years, you may want to discuss any special coursework, honours, programs, or projects from high school.

_____

_____

JOB DESCRIPTION ACTIVITY

Before you write the job description for your résumé, try your hand at this exercise. It is designed to provide the opportunity to practise some creative thinking about jobs you've held.

Directions

Use your personal list of action verbs and your imagination to create some innovative job descriptions for the positions outlined below. Background information for each job is provided. Pay special attention to the use of action verbs. Remember that present tense jobs are described with phrases beginning with present tense verbs. Remember to keep descriptions of your previous jobs in the past tense.

Example

You worked at Carlson's Café for three years while you were attending college. Your title was assistant restaurant manager and your responsibilities included managing a staff of 10 servers, scheduling work days for your staff, taking care of any problems or disagreements that occurred with staff members or patrons, running the cash register and fixing it when broken, doing the banking of receipts, and training new servers as they were hired.

If you were writing a creative job description for this example, here's how it might look:

- Trained and managed a staff of 10 employees
- Handled scheduling of server staff
- Provided friendly and prompt customer service
- Operated and repaired electronic cash register
- Handled over $1500 in cash receipts per day
- Communicated with restaurant staff and ownership to improve restaurant operations

....

See what you can do with the following situations.
Don't forget to use those action verbs effectively!

Situation #1

You have worked for several years as a technical writer for a software company. Your duties include taking programming notes and converting them into plain English for user documents. You are also responsible for creating appropriate graphics using several desktop publishing programs, soliciting printing quotes from local printers, and handling ordering and distribution of manuals and documents. You also create marketing brochures for the sales staff and occasionally are called upon to assist in other company promotional programs.

Description #1

_____

_____

_____

_____

_____

Situation #2

You work as owner and manager of a daycare centre located in a mid-sized town. You recruit and hire qualified daycare providers, you manage the day-to-day operations of the centre, you handle provincial licensing and compensation paperwork, and you plan, purchase, and prepare food for your staff and the children. Additionally, you plan special interest programs in art, music, and physical education for the children. You are implementing a "Computer for Kids" program that will be a model for centres across the province.

Description #2

_____

_____

_____

_____

_____

Situation #3

You currently work as a telemarketer in an environment which provides minimal supervision. You are responsible for keeping accurate records of the calls you make as well as tracking the outcome of each call. You were named "Employee of the Month" when you organized a mini-workshop for your coworkers on how to handle difficult customers. Your supervisor sometimes calls upon you to substitute for her. You volunteer to work extra hours when coworkers are sick. You have consistently scored as one of the top two salespersons for your telemarketing division.

Description #3

_____

_____

_____

_____

_____

Using the job you currently hold (or the last one held), write a detailed paragraph describing the position situation and the duties and tasks associated with that position. After you have finished the descriptive paragraph, write a creative job description for the same position that would be suitable for inclusion in your résumé. Remember to use action verbs and supply the correct verb tense. Write the job title below.

Job Title _____

Situation

_____

_____

_____

_____

_____

_____

Description

_____

_____

_____

_____

_____

_____

_____

_____

_____

_____

_____

_____

Now that you have the practise, write a description for all the positions you intend to put in your résumé. If necessary, review your lists of action verbs. Don't be shy about any of your accomplishments!

Now that you have finished with advice on résumé writing, let's look at some samples. Remember, how you organize and lay out your résumé on the page is just as subjective as what you choose to put into it. You need to decide what looks the best to you and what showcases your traits and skills most appropriately. Also, remember that your résumé needs to be attractive and easy to read.

SAMPLE RÉSUMÉS

SAMPLE CHRONOLOGICAL RÉSUMÉ

RYAN H. SANDERS
1221 Pleasant Hill Drive
Toronto, ON   M5P 2T9
416-495-8892
rsanders@linkup.com

EDUCATION

June 1998

COMPUTER PROGRAMMER ANALYST - GRADUATE
Lambton College, Sarnia, ON

Honours:

GPA 3.90/4.00
Dean's Honour List
Computer Science Honour Society

QUALIFICATIONS

- programmed various applications using COBAL, CICS, PASCAL, AS400
- assembler on IBM O/S
- French bilingual

WORK EXPERIENCE

1996 – present

Operations supervisor
SPEEDY PARCEL SERVICE CORPORATION, Toronto, ON

- Responsible for controlling production, efficiency, employee motivation, promotion and discipline
- Supervise 25 floor employees during second shift
- Train new employees, hold communications meetings
- Evaluate employees in performance reviews

Sept – Dec 1997

Co-op
ABC AUTOMOTIVE PARTS, Toronto, ON

- Served as project leader for co-op consulting project
- Designed and implemented an inventory tracking system for automotive parts dealers
- Gained experience with DBASE 11 and Masterfile programs

1994 – 1996

Destination Specialist
GROUND DELIVERY TRANSPORTATION, Toronto, ON

- Consulted with clients concerning systems operation
- Advised technical managers in operational techniques
- Conducted oral presentations for internal and external audiences

REFERENCES

Available upon request

SAMPLE FUNCTIONAL RÉSUMÉ

RYAN H. SANDERS
1221 Pleasant Hill Drive
Toronto, ON   M5P 2T9
416-495-8892
rsanders@linkup.com

EDUCATION   **COMPUTER PROGRAMMER ANALYST - GRADUATE** June 1998
Lambton College, Sarnia, ON

Honours: GPA 3.90/4.00
Dean's Honour List
Computer Science Honour Society

SKILLS
Supervisory:
- Responsible for controlling production, efficiency, employee motivation, promotion, and discipline
- Supervisor of 25 floor employees during second shift
- Project leader for co-op consulting project

Technical:
- Programmed various applications using COBAL, CICS, PASCAL, AS400
- Assembler on IBM O/S
- Analyzed and designed systems case studies
- Designed and implemented an inventory tracking system for automotive parts distributor
- Experienced with DBASE 11 and Masterfile programs

Communication:
- Consulted with clients concerning systems operation
- Advised technical managers in operational techniques
- Trained new employees and held communications meetings
- Evaluated employees in job performance reviews
- Conducted oral presentations for internal and external audiences
- French bilingual

EMPLOYMENT

Operations Supervisor, April 1996 – present
SPEEDY PARCEL SERVICE CORPORATION, Toronto, ON

Co-op, Sept – Dec 1997
ABC AUTOMOTIVE PARTS, Toronto, ON

Destination Specialist, 1994 – 1996
GROUND DELIVERY TRANSPORTATION, Toronto, ON

REFERENCES   Available upon request

SAMPLE COMBINATION RÉSUMÉ

RYAN H. SANDERS

416-495-8892

1221 Pleasant Hill Drive, Toronto, ON   M5P 2T9

rsanders@linkup.com

OBJECTIVE	**COMPUTER PROGRAMMER ANALYST**

PERSONAL SUMMARY

- Experienced supervisor, problem-solver and data processor
- Knowledge of a variety of computer languages and software programs
  - COBAL, CICS, PASCAL, AS400, assembler on IBM O/S
- Possess excellent communication, organization and managerial skills
  - French bilingual
- Self-motivated and loyal individual

EDUCATION

June 1998

COMPUTER PROGRAMMER ANALYST - GRADUATE
Lambton College, Sarnia, ON

Honours

GPA 3.90/4.00
Dean's Honour List
Computer Science Honour Society

WORK EXPERIENCE

1996 – present

Operations Supervisor
SPEEDY PARCEL SERVICE CORPORATION, Toronto, ON

- Responsible for controlling production, efficiency, employee motivation, promotion and discipline
- Supervise 25 floor employees during second shift
- Train new employees, hold communications meetings
- Evaluate employees in performance reviews

Sept – Dec 1997

Co-op
ABC AUTOMOTIVE PARTS, Toronto, ON

- Served as project leader for co-op consulting project
- Designed and implemented an inventory tracking system for automotive parts dealers
- Gained experience with DBASE 11 and Masterfile programs

1994 – 1996

Destination Specialist
GROUND DELIVERY TRANSPORTATION, Toronto, ON

- Consulted with clients concerning systems operation
- Advised technical managers in operational techniques
- Conducted oral presentations for internal and external audiences

REFERENCES

Available upon request

TWO PAGE RÉSUMÉ

JEFFREY GAMBO
11245 Greenbrook Lane Apt. 12, Kitchener, ON   N2L 3H5
519-242-0047
gambo@ebtech.net

OBJECTIVE	Electronics position to utilize electronic, communication and mechanical skills

EDUCATION

1996

ELECTRONICS ENGINEERING TECHNOLOGY DIPLOMA
Conestoga College, Kitchener ON
GPA 3.70/4.00

QUALIFICATIONS

- Digital analysis
- Microprocessors
- C Programming
- Solid state devices
- Control systems
- W.H.M.I.S.
- Windows 98, Microsoft Office, Internet research, e-mail
- Excellent proven customer service skills
- Supervisory experience

EXPERIENCE

1998 – present

Service Technician
FIELDTECH INC., Kitchener, ON
- Perform field service on wide variety of equipment
- Troubleshoot and repair sophisticated medical equipment
- Install multimillion dollar diagnostic equipment
- Work efficiently and accurately under pressure and with little or no supervision

1996 – 1998

Assistant Supervisor
MARTIN IMAGE COMPANY, Cambridge, ON
- Supervised 10 repair personnel
- Coordinated work schedules
- Trained new employees
- Provided customer service
- Assisted with outside sales
- Ran diagnostic tests on electronic equipment

Jeffrey Gambo   **519 242 0047**

1994 – 1996   **Customer Service Representative**
                            ELECTRONICS R US, Kitchener, ON
- Sales of electronic and home entertainment products
- Provided excellent customer service
- Consistently met monthly sales targets

VOLUNTEER

BIG BROTHERS, Kitchener, ON
- Big Brother to 10-year-old
- Active fundraiser for Big Brothers

CANADIAN CANCER SOCIETY
- Door-to-door canvasser
- Participate in community fundraising events

INTERESTS

- Active in team sports including hockey and baseball
- Work out to maintain physical fitness
- photography

OTHER SAMPLE FORMAT

CAROLYN STEVENSON
492 Middleton Lane
Calgary, AB   T0M 3Y5
403-430-3758

PROFESSIONAL SUMMARY

Areas of strength in accounting include:
- Cost Accounting, Federal Tax Accounting, Accounting Information Systems
- Word for Windows, Dbase 11, DacEasy computerized accounting package

Take pride in producing accurate calculation for data used by management for budgeting, forecasting, and sales projections. Capable of building excellent working relationships with professional staffs at all levels.

Decision-making and leadership skills used to prioritize daily workload. Organize projects and written reports and records. Consistent follow-up on work environment to ensure meeting deadlines on time and to specifications.

EMPLOYMENT

Tax Associate   1996 – present
CLARK AND LEWIS ACCOUNTING SERVICE, Calgary AB
- Perform tax compliance, analysis, and research for consolidated companies
- Provide tax consulting to partnerships, trustee, and non-profit organization
- Awarded excellent rating for customer service

Accounting Assistant   1994 – 1996
ASPEN HILL RETIREMENT COMMUNITY, Windsor ON
- Responsible for developing and presenting financial topics to residents
- Counselled individuals concerning personal finances on a one-to-oe Director of Accounting for the community
- Provided assistance to Corporate Controller in financial statement matters

EDUCATION

Bachelor of Commerce,   1994
University of Windsor, Windsor ON

Accounting Diploma   1992
Lambton College, Sarnia ON

References available upon request

RÉSUMÉ CHECKLIST

Now that you have completed this section on the résumé and have seen some examples, it is time to create or update your own. Whether you developed yours by yourself or with the help of a computer program, use the following as a final check before you get ready to print your copies.

Overall Appearance

_____ Are all the margins equal and does your résumé appear balanced on the page?

_____ Is the content consistent in such things as capitalization, verb tense, and punctuation?

_____ Are your key points either at the left margins or on the top half of the sheet?

_____ Does your name stand out, and are your address and phone number correct?

Career Objective

_____ If you have included this section, is the objective original and have you indicated what you are able to contribute to the company, as well as what you would like to gain?

_____ Have you tried to be as specific as possible without limiting yourself too much?

_____ Did you put your statement in the third person and not use "my" or "I?"

Personal Summary

_____ Have you briefly described your accomplishments?

_____ Have you included specific personal skills?

_____ Have you included any experience with current electronic technologies?

Qualifications

_____ Have you listed your computer skills including software you are experienced using?

_____ Have you included any special training courses?

_____ Have you included any valid certificates or licenses such as C.P.R. or W.H.M.I.S.?

_____ Have you included all relevant skills that may not have been mentioned elsewhere?

_____ Have you included any professional memberships that may be relevant?

Education

_____ Have you included the name and city and province of your school?

_____ Have you included the correct title of your degree/diploma and date it was granted? If a recent graduate, have you included your GPA?

_____ Have you included any special learning circumstances such as a consulting internship, or extensive laboratory experience?

_____ Have you included any pertinent extracurricular activities?

_____ Have you included any computer hardware, software, or any other experience with special equipment?

Work Experience

_____ Have you included the names of the companies where you have been employed as well as the cities and provinces in which they are located?

_____ Have you included the terms of your positions, including the months and years?

_____ Have you remembered to include the titles of your positions?

_____ When you discussed your job responsibilities, were you descriptive and did you use transferable skills and action verbs whenever possible?

_____ Check through your job descriptions; do all the verb tenses agree with the time that the positions were held (i.e., all past tense verbs for past positions)?

_____ Did you leave out managers' names and any mention of salary or reasons for leaving?

Personal

_____ If you have included this section, have you made the information meaningful and useful to your job search? (You may want to include comments on relocation, travel, future educational plans, interesting hobbies, etc.).

INTERNET RÉSUMÉ SITES

The following is a listing of some interesting locations on the Internet for further tips, examples, advice, etc. and our comments on these sites. **Please remember this: Sites on the Internet change constantly; therefore, some of the addresses below may be relocated or may have disappeared by the time you read this. Also, the listing of Internet sites in this book in no way indicates recommendations or endorsements by Prentice Hall or by the authors. These are listed for information only.**

CACEE - Canadian Association of Career Educators and Employers
www.cacee.com/
Résumé tips, Online magazines, new trends and more.

Career Centre Résumé Topics
www.jobweb.org/catapult/jsguides.htm
Interesting résumé samples with many links to résumé and other job search sites.

College Grad Job Hunter
www.collegegrad.com
Best college résumés, Internet résumé postings and database resources.

Get Wired, You're Hired
www.wiredhired.com
The Canadian Guide to job hunting on-line.

Job Hunters Bible
www.jobhuntersbible.com/
From the author of What Color is Your Parachute.

The Riley Guide
www.dbm.com/jobguide/
Loaded with tips résumé and Internet info.

QUESTIONS

REVIEW QUESTIONS

1. What are the three basic type of résumés discussed in the chapter?

2. What is the recommended length for résumés used by recent graduates?

3. What type of writing style is appropriate for résumé writing?

4. What determines the amount of detail to be used in the education section of a résumé?

5. What's the difference between a duty statement and a scope statement in the work experience section of a résumé?

6. The Personal/Professional Summary section of a résumé includes what type of information?

7. What is an electronic résumé?

8. List three tips for creating scannable résumés.

DISCUSSION QUESTIONS

1. Under what circumstances would a functional résumé be appropriate? If you were to create a functional résumé, do you think recruiters would be attracted to it because of its uniqueness or ignore it because it may be different from many others?

2. What is your view on putting a personal section in the résumé? What are its advantages and disadvantages?

3. Considering the three different types of résumé, which would be best suited for a homemaker or a semi-retired individual who is looking to re-enter the work force after several years' absence? Defend your choice.

4. Differences of opinion exist today on the advantages of résumé scanning software. Some feel the automated approach is good, saves times, and is objective. Others feel because it is too high tech, it is low touch or impersonal and takes important decisions out of the hands of people. What is your view?

4 REFERENCES:

Kind Words From Friends

Do I need to have references? Will they be checked? How many should I have? Whom should I select? What should they say about me? Many questions like these come up when thinking about references for a job search. Companies differ in their requirements for references. Some will want them after the first interview or two. Others will want them at the end of the interview process, but before they will consider making a job offer. Some will never ask for them! Some companies will even check references prior to the interview. So what should you do?

First of all, you **do** need references. You never know if the company you are interviewing with will require them or when they will be requested. So it is best to be prepared. If recruiters ask you for references, they will probably be checked. It is not efficient to check references by mail, so telephone calls are most often the way that references will be contacted. Following are some answers to frequently asked questions on references.

How many references should I have?
Many people use between three to five individuals. Some may be personal references and others may be professional ones.

Whom should I ask?
References usually fall into three categories: managers or supervisors, professional contacts (coworkers or business associates), personal friends (not family). You need to decide how many you want in each category; focus on work-related individuals. As a student or recent graduate you may want to use a faculty member. Never use members of your immediate family and always select people who are articulate and fairly easy to get hold of!

What should they say about me?
It depends. Professional references will address your work ethic, the quality of your work, your personality on the job, and similar qualities. Personal references will be asked about your character, personality in general, etc.

When should I provide references?
This information varies greatly depending on whom you speak to. Many experts suggest putting "References available upon request" at the bottom of your résumé. You would then take your references to an interview or wait for the potential employer to ask you for them. This is in fact the most common practice.

However you need to remember that the purpose is for you to secure employment by providing the relevant information to sell yourself. Certainly references are part of this process and providing them upfront indicates you are well prepared in your application. It also provides additional insight to the employer as well as making it easier to hire you.

If your references are not needed at this time at the very least your application is complete.

What other advice can you give on handling references?

Make a list of all your references for your own use. Have a second list of references on quality paper to give to potential employers. See page 52 for a sample format for your reference sheet.

Get permission from your intended references before you give their names to prospective employers. Remember, you are asking these people to assist you in your job search. You want to be courteous about it, and you want them to be prepared. Tell your references about your job targets or your goals and make them aware of your most marketable traits. Also tell them about any specific calls from employers that they may receive.

Determine which references will be most appropriate for you. You need to select people who are willing and eager to brag about you! At the same time, you need to select people who can converse easily and are able to handle potentially difficult questions. Remember, people need to be available to receive phone calls about you: Don't select someone who is always out of town or in meetings.

Be careful not to overuse people who have agreed to be your references. It may be useful to select two individuals as your key references and rotate their names to the top of your reference list. Also, call your references to let them know each time you give their names to potential employers. Tell them to expect the calls.

Some final advice on dealing with job references includes a caution against striving for prestige rather than knowledge in your references. Don't pick someone who has an impressive title or position but very little knowledge about you. Finally, remember to thank the people who have served as your references. It also might be a good idea to give progress reports on your new job to references who have helped you secure that position.

Currently, most reference inquiries are done by telephone. If you wish, you may want to include day and evening phone numbers for references, but first make sure this is acceptable to your references. No need to include e-mail addresses; employers still want to talk to others about potential employers, not read a message.

QUESTIONS YOUR REFERENCES MAY BE ASKED

A final tool to help you in selecting and preparing your references is a list of potential questions that references are often asked. Questions below are more typically asked of professional references; however, similar ones may be asked of personal references as well.

1. What is your relationship to the candidate?
2. How long have you known the candidate?
3. When and why did he/she leave the job?
4. Was the candidate absent from work? On time?
5. What were his/her duties?
6. How was the candidate's cooperation with supervisors and co-workers?
7. What are the attributes of the candidate?
8. What are the liabilities of the candidate?
9. Was he/she self-motivated?
10. Would you rehire the candidate if you had the opportunity?

Potential employers may also ask the reference to confirm information given on the résumé or job application.

REFERENCE SHEET

REFERENCES FOR
(YOUR NAME)

Professional

Name, title
Company
Company address
Telephone number(s)

Name, title
Company
Company address
Telephone number(s)

Name, title
Company
Company address
Telephone number(s)

Personal

Name
Address
Telephone number(s)

Name
Address
Telephone number(s)

QUESTIONS

1. Are references really necessary? Why?

2. How many references should you have?

3. When is the best time to give an employer your references?

1. If a person has agreed to be your reference, do you think it is necessary to call him or her each time he or she may be receiving a call about you? Why or why not?

2. Do you think it is fair for references to be asked about a candidate's absence record or the individual's liabilities? Why or why not?

CHAPTER
OBJECTIVES

After completing this chapter, you will:

Understand basic techniques of good letter writing.

Write an effective cover letter.

Produce other types of job search correspondence.

COVER LETTER ADVICE

5 LETTERS:

Cornerstone of Job Search Communication

A successful job search cannot be conducted without a focus on the correspondence that's a key part of securing a position. When are letters necessary? Quite often. First, there are the cover letters that will accompany your résumés. There are also the networking letters, the prospecting letters, the followup letters after the interview, and finally (and happily) the acceptance letter. Let's begin with one of the most important pieces of correspondence, the cover letter.

A cover letter, or letter of application as it is sometimes called, is the letter that covers your résumé, literally. This is the letter that is placed directly over the résumé and placed in the envelope. A cover letter introduces you to the potential employer. It makes a first impression, and it serves to set the tone for your résumé. Another useful purpose of the cover letter is that it can contain useful information that you choose not to place in your résumé. It can also spotlight something of importance that does appear in your résumé. So, all in all, it is a pretty important piece of writing. Let's take a look at the characteristics of a good cover letter. It does the following:

- Makes a good first impression and should always be original
- May involve several drafts before you get it the way you want it
- Is written on paper that will match the paper of the résumé
- Is one page in length or less
- Is direct and to the point (readers will not spend much time on them)
- Always provides an answer to the question "Why should I hire you?"

As was stated earlier, a cover letter must be well written. Its purpose is to transmit and present your résumé to a recruiter. It must put your very best foot forward. Essentially, cover letters can be written in three or four basic paragraphs:

1. The Introductory Paragraph where you apply for the position giving its title and how you learned about it.

2. The Middle Paragraph which references your résumé and sells you by mentioning your key attributes or traits. This paragraph may often be broken into two paragraphs to highlight separate areas such as work experience and education.

3. The Closing Paragraph which asks for the interview and indicates the follow up you will provide.

These three parts of a successful cover letter are shown on the next page using a typical letter format. Following this general example are samples of the following letters:

- Cover
- Application
- Networking
- Prospecting
- Thank you
- Acceptance

GUIDE FOR WRITING A COVER LETTER

1412 Ontario Street
Toronto, ON   M5P 1L6
March 21, 2000

Mr. Jerry P. Smith, Vice President
Lakewood General Hospital
545 Weller Avenue
Toronto, ON   M7N 2S3

Dear Mr. Smith:

Introductory Paragraph: In this paragraph, give the reason for the letter, name the specific position or type of employment for which you are applying, and mention how you learned about the opening.

The Middle Paragraphs: Indicate why you are interested in the position and company. Also state what you believe you can do for the company, what contributions you can make to it. If you are a recent graduate, talk about your degree and how you feel that it and your other experiences make you qualified for the position. If you are an experienced worker, point out your achievement or talents that make you a good candidate. You may be including some ideas similar to ones found in your résumé, but try not to use the very same wording. Finally, at the appropriate spot in this paragraph, refer the reader to your enclosed résumé, which further explains your qualifications and experience. This information is usually easier to separate into two paragraphs.

The Closing Paragraph: Here you thank the reader, and state your desire for an interview and your flexibility as to the time and place. You should include telephone numbers where you can be reached as well. As far as indicating what follow up you will take, it is highly recommended that you be assertive and active in the closing of the letter and tell the reader that you will be following up with a telephone call to arrange an interview time. You may also end the letter in a more passive way with a basic statement that you look forward to hearing from the reader; however, the only place that gets you is sitting by the telephone waiting for it to ring! Have more control than that; tell the reader when you will call and then do it!

Sincerely yours,

William H. Austin

Enclosure

SAMPLE BASIC COVER LETTER

34 Millbank Drive
London, ON   N2L 7X7

July 29, 2000

Ms. Jennifer Kutkowski
Senior Employment Specialist
Apex Communication Company
London, ON   N5P 1X7

Dear Ms. Kutkowski:

In response to your advertisement in the July 25th issue of *Communications Monthly*, I am applying for the position of network administrator. I would welcome the opportunity to be a part of your growing communications company.

During the past several years, I have developed excellent skills in network administration, working with our local television station, CLPL-TV. I have a broad knowledge of network operations as well as an understanding of the complexities of managing a system in a company such as yours. I was very excited to see your advertisement for someone with my skills.

Thank you for reviewing my enclosed résumé. I look forward to meeting with you so that we can further discuss your exciting opportunity and my related qualifications. I will contact you next week so that we may arrange a convenient time to meet.

Sincerely,

James Herrman

Enclosure

Application Letter

The next letter is a variation on the cover letter. Similar to the letter that covers the résumé, the purpose of this type of correspondence is to apply for a position. If it is sent by itself, it is an application letter. If a résumé is enclosed with it, it becomes a cover letter. You'll notice that this letter is a bit more involved than the basic cover letter sample. The level of detail in this letter makes it much more appropriate for use as a singular letter of application. Most employers do expect a résumé to be included.

SAMPLE APPLICATION LETTER

1225 Hampton Avenue
Edmonton, AB   T8L 2N5

March 12, 2000

Mr. Derik C. Stephenson
Director of Human Resources
Peterson Industries
1345 West Edmonton Mall Road
Edmonton, AB   T9C 3S9

Dear Mr. Stephenson:

I am applying for the position of systems analyst which was advertised on March 10th with the placement service at St. Anne's College. The position is an excellent match with my education, experience, and career interests.

In your advertisement, you ask for experience in computers systems, financial applications software, and end-user consulting. With a major in management information systems, I have training on mainframes, mini- and micro-computers. I also have training and experience with a variety of software programs and applications. My hands-on experience as a computer laboratory assistant at St. Anne's and as a programmer and student assistant has given me valuable exposure to various hardware and software problems as well as situations requiring good interpersonal communications skills. In addition, I have been employed as a student worker with a large credit union, where I gained valuable knowledge of financial systems. My experience and career goals match your requirements well. I am extremely interested in the systems analyst position and in working for Peterson Industries.

Please consider my request for an interview to discuss further my qualifications and to present you with a résumé detailing my educational and work experiences. I will call you next week to see if a meeting can be arranged. If you would like to reach me before then, please call me at 403-665-7828. If I am not in, please leave a message, and I will return your call within a day. Thank you for your consideration. I look forward to meeting and talking with you.

Sincerely,

Charles S. Parsons

Charles S. Parsons

Enclosure

CHAPTER 5 • LETTERS

Networking Letter

Networking letters can be an important part of your job search. This type of correspondence can increase your number of contacts and help you find people to help you in your job search. In a later chapter, we will discuss the critical importance that networking has in your job search. But for now, let's see what a networking letter looks like.

SAMPLE NETWORKING LETTER

2929 Appleton Court
Woodstock, ON   N6P 3L5

October 20, 2000

Ms. Marlene Walker, Director
Jones, Walker, and Smith
1400 Commerce Dr. Suite 201
London, ON   N7P 5B6

Dear Ms. Walker:

Dr. Myron Olsen, professor of law at the University of Western Ontario and a personal friend of my parents, suggested that I contact you. He thought that you, as a corporate lawyer, might be in an excellent position to assist me with a decision relating to my career.

As a law student, I am exploring different paths of employment. Corporate law, media law, and tax and financial law all sound interesting to me at this point, but I want to begin my job search next term with a clearer sense of understanding of these options. I would like to get your opinion of these areas and get a glimpse of a corporate law office in action.

I will be calling you next week to see if we can arrange a brief meeting at your convenience. Thank you for considering my request.

Sincerely,

Janet R. Counsel

Janet R. Counsel

Prospecting Letter

Sending prospecting letters is one method you can use to get your name and your qualifications in front of a variety of people. Generally, these letters are used when there is no clear or advertised opening, yet you have interest in the company and would like to send a letter to check out your "prospect." While your job search should not be composed only of prospecting letters, they can be useful in enhancing your chances of getting hired. The first example of a prospecting letter is structured more as a letter résumé, while the second example is a prospecting cover letter that would accompany a résumé.

SAMPLE PROSPECTING LETTER

10 Sussex Drive
Ottawa, ON   P3Z 5K2

January 4, 2001

Mr. John Jenkins, President
POWERCO Incorporated
733 Parliament Road
Ottawa, ON   P3L 7N3

Dear Mr. Jenkins:

In my six years as General Marketing Manager of a prominent construction distributor in suburban Ottawa, I managed the sales and leasing matters for power equipment for medium to heavy construction equipment.

During that time:
- Annual billing of sales and rental increased from $1.2 million to $4.8 million.
- Profits rose dramatically from my first to my second year in charge of billing.
- The number of accounts increased more than 120%.

My success in these and other sales and marketing endeavours was due to creativity, hard work, and perseverance. My degree in Business Operations combined with my natural ability to read various selling situations has been key to my successes. My innovative programs have contributed to the bottom-line profits of the firms for which I have worked.

I would be happy to meet with you so we can discuss how I might be of service to your company. I will call next week so we can arrange a mutually convenient time for us to get together.

Sincerely,

Sydney Sullivan

Enclosure

SAMPLE PROSPECTING LETTER

850 Baldwin Avenue
Ridgetown, ON   N0P 2C0

December 12, 2000

Mr. Tony Lawrence
Director of College Recruiting
Northern Apple Association
1232 University Avenue
Toronto, ON   M5L 6P9

Dear Mr. Lawrence:

I read about your company in a recent issue of *The Globe and Mail* and would like to inquire into employment opportunities in your sales trainee program. I want to work in retail sales and management and would like to relocate to Toronto after graduation.

I will receive my BA degree in June. I have always been interested in sale opportunities and held a variety of sales and marketing positions in high school and college. My internship with a large department store convinced me that sales and marketing were the fields for me. As I read about your company, I was convinced that you provide the kind of professional retail environment that I seek.

My résumé is enclosed for your review. I would appreciate a few minutes of your time to further discuss my qualifications and possible opportunities within your firm. I shall call you during the next week. Thank you for considering my request.

Sincerely,

Craig Bandeau

Enclosure

Thank You Letter

Every successful job search has one thing in common: The job seeker spent time in following up and following through. Developing skills lists, updating résumés, even having a good cover letter won't benefit you if you don't follow up on contacts and interviews. Employers expect it. In fact, a recruiter once commented that he did not even bother to call back anyone who did not contact him after the interview. Recruiters want to know that you want them. They expect you to assert yourself without being obnoxious. One way to accomplish this is to make sure you send thank you letters after each and every time you interview. More will be mentioned about this in the chapter on interviewing. For now, let's examine a typical thank you letter.

SAMPLE THANK YOU LETTER

1225 Hampton Avenue
Edmonton, AB   T8L 2N5

April 20, 2001

Mr. Derik C. Stephenson
Director of Human Resources
Peterson Industries
1345 West Edmonton Mall Road
Edmonton, AB   T9C 3S9

Dear Mr. Stephenson:

I want to thank you very much for the opportunity to interview with you yesterday for the position of systems analyst. I really enjoyed meeting you and learning more about your consulting operations and financial records systems.

As I stated in the interview, the requirements for your position and my qualifications are a match. I have training and experience with the systems you use, plus I have excellent communications skills and can deal effectively with individuals on a variety of levels. I'm certain that I would fit into your team and will ultimately make a significant contribution to your firm.

I want to stress again my strong interest in your position and your organization. Thank you for your continued consideration.

Sincerely,

Charles S. Parsons

Charles S. Parsons

Acceptance Letter

The most joyful letter you may ever write is the acceptance letter. What is it and when is it used? An acceptance letter is sent to an individual in a company that has made you a job offer that you plan to accept. Many offers are made verbally, and it is always a good idea to have the particulars of the offer on paper. Therefore, if the potential employer does not put the offer in writing (either initially or as a follow up to the verbal offer), it is a good idea for you to draft an acceptance letter. There also may be times when the potential employer does put the offer in writing, and you may still wish to respond with your own acceptance letter. Let's see what one of these happy letters looks like.

SAMPLE ACCEPTANCE LETTER

34 Millbank Drive
London, ON   N2L 7X7

July 29, 2000

Ms. Jennifer Kutkowski
Senior Employment Specialist
Apex Communication Company
London, ON   N5P 1X7

Dear Ms. Kutkowski:

I am writing to confirm my acceptance of your August 16th offer of the position of network administrator for Apex Communication. I am delighted that I will soon be joining your fine firm. I know I can contribute to your organization, and I appreciate the opportunity you have given me.

As we discussed on the 16th, I will report to work at 8:00 a.m. on Monday, August 24th and will have completed the required physical examination by that time. My starting salary will be $33 000 yearly, and I will receive a performance review after six months of service. I will be reporting to Mr. Harold White as one of his junior network administrators.

I look forward to working with Mr. White and being a part of Apex Communication. I will report to your office August 24th to fill in the required personnel forms. I look forward to seeing you soon.

Sincerely,

James Herrman

TIPS ON LETTER WRITING

Now that we have examined the various types of job search correspondence, there are a few final tips to keep in mind when creating this and any type of business correspondence. When typing the name of the recipient, use the proper identifier. The abbreviation "Mr." poses no problem because it is used for both married and unmarried men. "Miss" will work for an unmarried woman and "Mrs." is used for married women. If you are in doubt or don't care to make this type of distinction, use the abbreviation "Ms." This term is perfectly acceptable for both married and unmarried women because it is a standard abbreviation representing the word woman.

In addition to identifier, proper spelling is also very important. If you are uncertain as to the spelling of a person's name, call the company and tell them you want to make sure you have the correct spelling. Remember, even simple names like Smith or Johnson can be spelled different ways. Also concerning names, don't assume certain names are either masculine or feminine. Frances could be a man, and Taylor could be a woman. Call to make sure. Also, if the reader of your letter has a title, use it. Most people like to see their names and titles in print, and they definitely want to see them spelled correctly!

Do you know why a letter has a typed signature at the end? This is included in case the recipient cannot read your signature. Whenever sending business correspondence make sure to sign your name above the typed signature. Also, if you are enclosing your résumé, be sure to type the word "Enclosure" underneath your name. This tells the reader that there is something else in the envelope with the letter. Also, as you did with the résumé make sure everything is correct in your letters. Punctuate correctly and check carefully for misspellings and typographical errors.

Finally, it is a good idea to keep copies of all your job search correspondence. When you are in the middle of a busy job search campaign, it will be helpful to review items you have sent. Keep photocopies of your letters or make sure you have saved them on your computer.

QUESTIONS

1. What is the function of a cover letter?

2. In which paragraph of the cover letter should you sell yourself?

3. What word do you need to type at the bottom of a cover letter to indicate that something else is included with it?

4. Why are networking letters important?

5. What does an acceptance letter do for you?

1. If a potential employer is primarily interested in your résumé why send a cover letter at all?

2. Why is it recommended that cover letters end with an active statement? Why not just wait until the employer calls you?

3. In this age of faxes, e-mail, and Internet home pages, do you think it's necessary to have job search letter writing skills? Why or why not?

6 JOB APPLICATIONS:

Techniques and Tips

In addition to résumés and letters, another written component of the job search process is the job application. Are they necessary to complete? In almost all cases the answer is yes. Most companies still use job applications and some must have completed applications on file before offers are extended. Because job applications are still a requirement for employment, you should be prepared to fill them out at any point in the job search process.

When you apply for a position, whether in person or through the mail, you may receive a job application. The application may be mailed to you, or you may be asked to complete it when you arrive for your first interview. No matter when asked to complete the application, there are some techniques to keep in mind.

To be ready to complete an application form, you may want to make sure you have a copy of your résumé with you or even a master application prepared in advance. Although you would not want to leave an application blank and write instructions to see your attached résumé, and although you could never submit your own prepared application to an employer, having a copy of your résumé on hand or having a master application filled in can save you time and help ensure accuracy when filling out the real thing.

BEFORE FILLING IT OUT

Before filling out the application, make sure you read it thoroughly, no matter how many you have filled out previously. Each company's application may be just a bit different, so pay attention. Fill out the application completely and honestly. Most applications have a space for your signature and the date at the end. Don't forget to sign it. Signing an application indicates that you testify to the completeness and accuracy of the document. Do not omit or misrepresent anything. Falsification of application information can be grounds for immediate dismissal.

GENERAL ADVICE

General advice for filling out applications includes printing clearly and not skipping sections or lines of the application. If a section or line doesn't apply to you, simply write NA for not applicable in the appropriate spaces or place a small line in that section or box. It is not necessary (and oftentimes difficult at best) to try to type your responses on an application. Some recruiters say that they notice how careful job candidates are when filling out applications. Be neat. Also, recruiters have said that they are interested in viewing personal handwriting, so make sure your writing is legible too! Below are five tips to keep in mind when preparing to fill out a job application.

FIVE TIPS

1. **Always use black or blue ink.**
   Although pencil can be erased, it smudges easily and is harder to read. Do not use a marker as it may bleed through.

2. **Check directions carefully.**
   Does the application ask you to print or write? What other specific directions does it give you? Remember to read the entire application over before writing.

3. **Spelling should be correct.**
   Be very careful; make sure you can spell all the terms and words connected to your work. Don't misspell names of companies. Don't guess at any spellings; be sure before you begin.

4. **Be careful how you handle sections on salary.**
   The best place to talk about salary is in an interview, not in an application. Therefore, it may be best to write the term "Open" or "Negotiable" if requested to indicate salary expectations. Any information on past salary history should be accurate.

5. **Practice makes perfect.**
   Practise by filling out the application on the following pages. Have it available at home or when applying for jobs so you can ensure accuracy, correctness, and neatness when you fill in the actual job application.

ACORN CELLULAR

Employment Application

Personal Information

Date _____

Name	Last	First		Middle	
Present Address	Street	City	Province	Postal Code	
Permanent Address	Street	City	Province	Postal Code	
Phone Number		**Referred By**			

Employment Desired

Position	Date You Can Start	Salary Desired
Are You Presently Employed?	If So, May We Inquire of Your Present Employer?	

Education

	Name & Location of School	Years Attended	Date Graduated	Major/Program
Post-secondary				
Trade, Business or Correspondence				
High School				

General

Subjects of special study or research work
What foreign languages do you speak fluently?   Read?   Write?
Are you legally eligible to accept employment in Canada? ☐ Yes ☐ No

Work Related Skills

Describe any relevent skills, certificates, licenses, or training.

Former Employers (List below last four employers starting with last one first)

Date/Month/Year	Employer Name and Address	Salary	Position	Reason For Leaving
From To				
Responsibilities				
From To				
Responsibilities				
From To				
Responsibilities				
From To				
Responsibilities				

References (Give below the names of three persons not related to you whom you have known at least one year)

Name	Address	Business	Years Known

I authorize investigation of all statements contained in this application. I understand that misrepresentation or omission of facts called for is cause for dismissal.

Signature	Date

QUESTIONS

1. Are job applications necessary? Why?

2. Why is it a good idea to use your résumé and perhaps a pre-prepared application when filling out the real thing?

3. What should you do if a part or section of an application does not pertain to you?

4. Why shouldn't you use a pencil when you fill out an application?

1. Can you include facts on an application that are different from facts on your résumé? Why or why not?

2. If you have a criminal record, this should never be put on an application, even if it has a question asking about criminal convictions. True or False? Justify your answer.

*After completing this
chapter, you will:*

*Understand the benefits of
good company research.*

*Determine what types of
information to gather on
companies.*

*Be able to research
company information both
traditionally and
electronically.*

⁊ COMPANY RESEARCH:

The Why's & How's

In the book *Researching Your Way to a Good Job*, Karmen N. T. Crowther gives an excellent rationale as to why you need to research a company. Chances are when you send out your résumé, and when you go to an employment interview, you know little about the organization that may become your employer. Perhaps you know the company's address and that it makes lawn mowers or computer chips, but do you know anything more? Do you know if the company is financially stable, has a reputation for quality products and service, or is interested in innovation? Does the company offer its employees opportunities for growth and promotion? Are long-term prospects for its industry good? These are questions that deserve to be researched.

Most books for job seekers begin with advice about the résumé and cover letter. These two documents typically serve as a company's first impression of an applicant. If the impression is a good one, an invitation to a job interview may follow. Job search experts often mention the importance of researching a company before going to an interview, maybe even before sending out the résumé and cover letter. The advice, however, is usually brief enough to overlook. Can anything covered in only a page or two be as important as the résumé or interview? The answer: *Yes, researching a company is important.* Learning about a prospective employer is basic to creating an appropriate résumé and cover letter. It is fundamental to a successful interview and, most important, is central to establishing a mutually successful and enduring work relationship. Often overlooked, company research is the job search step this chapter will explore.

WHAT ARE THE BENEFITS OF RESEARCHING A COMPANY?

Most job hunters select potential employers haphazardly. They scan job advertisements in newspapers or professional publications and send out inquiries to any company that seeks someone with their qualifications. Others sign up for open interviews with any company whose recruiters are passing through their locality, or they canvas their friends and colleagues for leads. Still others send out dozens, even hundreds, of inquiry letters to a list of companies drawn from a telephone directory, hoping that their letter will reach a personnel officer's hands just as a vacancy occurs. In each of these situations, the job hunter knows little, if anything, about the companies that respond. The chances of being satisfied with an employer selected in this manner are poor. Although the fit between job hunter and employer may turn out well, the chances are slim. Still, these hit-or-miss techniques are used again and again. Following are four excellent reasons why you need to invest some time in researching employers.

HELP IN SELECTING PROSPECTIVE EMPLOYERS

What if you use a different approach? Instead of leaving the initial decision making to the employer, take the initiative yourself. Assemble a list of position vacancies and companies that you are interested in and then research each company using standard library sources, computer online sources, and networking with others. As you learn about a company's organizational climate, its reputation and future outlook, its products and financial condition, you will have a better basis for judging whether you might be content working on its staff. If your research reveals major drawbacks in a prospective employer, you've saved the price of mailing your résumé and possibly the time and disappointment of an unproductive interview. On the other hand, if your research turns up potential for a good match between a company's needs and prospects and your talents and aspirations, you have a good chance for a successful interview.

If you plan to send out a number of blind inquiries, preliminary research will be even more effective. Don't send out résumés to every engineering firm in Toronto or to all the advertising agencies in Vancouver. Apply a list of desired criteria to your company selection and you will create a more productive list of employment possibilities. Even if you consider only a firm's size or number of years in business, you will have made a start at evaluating characteristics that affect the company's current success and future viability. As you make your initial selections, you may also become aware that you have specific preferences about the kind of company for which you want to work.

BETTER COVER LETTERS AND RÉSUMÉS

One of the benefits of research is that you begin to see how you might fit into a company and what you can offer to it. This is especially important as you begin preparing a cover letter and résumé that will attract a company's attention and interest.

A good cover letter can establish your interest in the company and the position available, demonstrate the value you can bring to the organization, and highlight your strengths and abilities. If you can show in the first paragraph that you have a personal interest in the company or specific knowledge of its activities, it adds an individual touch that attracts the reader's attention. And the more you know about the company, the better you can target your comments about your own qualifications.

You also can tailor your résumé to a company's needs based on your research. For example, suppose you have experience in both marketing and advertising and presently work in the food industry. You discover a promising job opening in marketing, but with a leading pharmaceutical company. Your research indicates that the firm has recently begun to diversify into new areas, primarily food additives and nutritional supplements; the food industry will be a major focus of the company's future marketing strategies. Based on these facts, highlight the relevant aspects of your background and experience in your résumé, focusing on your marketing expertise and experience in the food industry, valuable attractions to this expanding firm.

MORE EFFECTIVE INTERVIEWS

Researching a prospective employer can help in preparing a cover letter and résumé that get the desired result — an interview. But how can your research affect the outcome of an interview? Based on what you learn, you will be able to respond to questions in a way that demonstrates the fit between your background and the company's needs. It will also demonstrate that you've done your homework.

Most books on job interviewing will suggest standard questions you should expect from the interviewer. Think through your answers to these questions. If you have studied the company as well as the questions, your answers will be on target. They will be based on the skills and experience you offer and your knowledge of the firm's current operations.

Often as the last step of an interview you will have an opportunity to ask questions. If you have done your homework, your research should reveal the key issues of interest or concern for any company you are considering as an employer. Through directed questions, you will be able to fill in the gaps in your research and to find out anything the interviewer may have overlooked when briefing you.

INFORMED EMPLOYMENT DECISIONS

If things have gone well, the moment you hoped for arrives. You are offered a position and must decide whether to accept. Once again, your research will pay off. Your impressions gained during the interview will be important, but review all that you have learned about the firm and its industry. Consider what you discovered in your background research and the facts added during your interview. If your evaluation leaves you with a positive assessment of the company and the position offered, or with only a few unresolved and insignificant questions, things look positive. Accept the position and enjoy your new job! Now that you have seen why it is important to research companies, let's explore some of the methods you can use.

WHAT COMPANY INFORMATION SHOULD YOU INVESTIGATE?

Both traditional and electronic sources can supply a vast wealth of information. In fact, oftentimes, it is hard to distinguish between what may be valuable for you to read and what may be nice but not necessary for your job search. Certainly you'll want to learn about the company's products or services and their finances; however, it may not be essential for you to learn that the company was founded in a garage by two young entrepreneurs or that the company has had twelve acquisitions in its 50-year history. On the other hand, it may be useful to learn what percent of their profit is returned to the company to fund research and development or how may times the company may have operated in the red. Here are some typical examples of useful company research information:

- Products and/or services and parent company and subsidiaries
- Relative size of the firm, its position in the industry, major competitors
- Geographic locations of parent company/subsidiaries
- Potential for growth of the firm and its industry as a whole
- Annual sales and/or profits for the last several years
- Organizational structure and management style or philosophy
- Corporate mission or vision statement
- Philosophy on training, development, and other employee programs

WAYS TO RESEARCH COMPANIES

Traditional Sources

Learning resource centres or libraries can be excellent places to get company information. Whether you are searching through a business, college, or community library, you may find a variety of sources in the reference section. Whatever resource books you choose to use, be sure to look at the beginning of the books to familiarize yourself with how they are organized. Also look through the indexes, because they can often tell you quickly whether the information you want is there. Some resource books have several indexes; check to see if resources have alphabetic listings of companies or arrangements of companies by industries or provinces. Some typical sources you may find in libraries include the following:

- *Blue Book of Canadian Business Profiles*
- *Canadian Almanac and Directory*
- *Canadian Key Business Directory*
- *Corporate Technology Directory*
- *Dun's Employment Opportunities Directory*
- *Fraser's Canadian Trade Directory*
- *Hoover's Guide to Computer Companies*
- *Hoover's Guide to Private Companies*
- *Hoover's Handbook of Emerging Companies*
- *Hoover's Masterlist*
- *Hoover's Handbook of World Business*
- *Jobs Hunter's Sourcebook*
- *Municipal Directory*
- *100 Best Jobs for 1990's and Beyond*
- *Scott's Industrial Directory*
- *Scott's Trade Directory*

Countless books have been published about various industries and companies: the best ones, who runs them, how to rate them, etc. Many of these books can be found in public libraries or bookstores. Some include titles such as:

- *The Career Directory 2000*
- *Best Jobs for the 21st Century*
- *Job Futures*
- *Jobs Rated Almanac*
- *100 Best Careers for the Year 2000*
- *100 Best Jobs for 1990's and Beyond*
- *Where the Jobs Are*
- *Who's Hiring 2000*

Other Printed Sources

Many sources of information can be obtained by means other than the library. If the company you are interested in learning about trades its stock on the stock market, it will have an annual report to stockholders and potential investors. These can be very good sources to read about a company and to take a look at its audited financial report. Many companies will send annual reports to interested parties through the mail. Some libraries and college placement offices may also have copies of annual reports of certain companies. If you look at annual reports on companies, remember that this is a biased piece of writing. Its purpose is to make the firm look good in the eyes of the audiences for which it is written. So, even though an annual report is a good source for an overview, it is also a source for a subjective view.

Major business periodicals, business newsletters, business newspapers, and general circulation newspapers often print articles about companies. These resources tend to be more objective in nature; however, they too may be presenting the company with a particular slant in mind. Regardless, it is highly recommended that you make a habit of regularly reading both business periodicals and the business sections of general circulation newspapers to keep on top of what companies are in the news.

Interviews

An excellent method of gathering firsthand information is interviews with individuals employed within various companies. Personnel departments, hiring authorities or various personal contacts can assist you in setting up these informational interviews. When attending informational interviews, a well-thought-through list of questions and some probing may net some interesting information. Also, when talking to individuals, answers to various questions can lead the information seeker to other questions to ask. Interviews can be a very interactive, useful and rewarding method of gathering information.

Electronic Sources

The way we gather information has changed dramatically in the last several years due to technology. An increasing number of companies are publishing information about themselves using electronic media. More and more individuals are finding that the computer is the preferred research tool. Many traditional paper resources are currently available on CD-ROM. In addition, many companies have locations on the Internet where detailed information about the firm, including lists of open positions, is available.

Internet Sources

Of all of the electronic sources at our command today, the Internet is probably the fastest-growing research tool. Its potential is truly amazing! More details on the Internet as part of your job search will be given later in this book, but let's look at some methods that can be used to capitalize on this powerful research tool.

Many companies today have a presence on the World Wide Web (WWW) in the form of home pages. A home page is a specific location or address on the Web where Internet users can obtain a wide variety of company information. Typical information on home pages include products and services offered, corporate mission statements, divisional offices, financial information, listing of staff with e-mail addresses, and even current job openings!

Try investigating to see if a company you are interested in is on the Web. If you are not an experienced Internet user, find someone to help you become one. When searching the Web for company information, try typing an address similar to the one below to get to a company's home page:

www.(name or abbreviation of company).com

An example of this would be www.motorola.com or www.intel.com. If this doesn't work, try going to one of the search engines such as Lycos, Yahoo Canada, or Alta Vista and searching under the company name.

The following are a few random Internet sites that you may find interesting and useful to explore. Again, more job search sites can be located by using various Internet search engines.

Campus Worklink: www.campusworklink.com
Jobs across Canada, campus work link, internship,links and more.

Canada Jobs: www.canadajobs.com
This site features Canadian and International resources, national companies and job postings.

Canada Work Info Net: www.workinfonet.ca
Career, education and labour market information.

Career Mosaic Canada: Canada.careermosaic.com
Many employers from high-technology industries are featured here in addition to a career resource centre, college connection, employer list, international employment options, and selected career articles and book reviews.

Human Resources Development Canada: www.hrdc-drhc.gc.ca
Quick path to job listings, work search help, résumé writing and workplace information.

Net Jobs: www.netjobs.com
Canadian employment site with links to company information.

The Monster Board: www.monster.ca
This famous and popular site includes job search information, résumé builders, employer profits, and online open houses for Canadians.

NOTE: Sites on the Internet change constantly. Therefore, some of the locations mentioned above may be relocated to different addresses or may have disappeared by the time you read this. Also, the listing of Internet sites in this book in no way indicates recommendation or endorsement by the author or the publisher. These references are informational only.

QUESTIONS

REVIEW QUESTIONS

1. List two of the four reasons for researching companies.

2. Give five examples of the type of material that needs to be researched concerning companies.

3. What is the difference between traditional and electronic sources?

DISCUSSION QUESTIONS

1. Review the information that should be investigated on p. 74. Which two or three areas for investigation do you think are the most important. Why?

2. What is an advantage that most electronic sources have over traditional ones?

CHAPTER
OBJECTIVES

*After completing this
chapter, you will:*

*Understand the importance
of networking in securing
employment.*

*Develop and use a network
planning sheet.*

*Use the most effective
methods to telemarket
yourself.*

*Be able to take advantage
of career fairs to increase
your marketability.*

8. NETWORKING, TELEMARKETING, CAREER FAIRS:

Fast Tracks to Employment

Now that you have done some self-analysis, worked through drafts and created a dynamic and good looking résumé, selected and notified your references, and have an understanding of the correspondence involved in a successful job search; there's one more very important ingredient — a job opening! How do you find out about openings? Where is the best place to look? According to many sources, the breakdown of how jobs are acquired looks something like this:

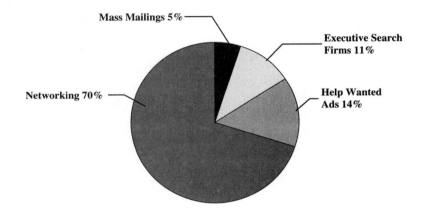

Mass Mailings 5%

Executive Search
Firms 11%

Help Wanted
Ads 14%

Networking 70%

What does this say about the most effective way to learn where the job are? While you should put some effort into answering help wanted or classified ads, conducting mass mailings, and even possibly using the services of search firms, the most effective way to learn about job openings is through networking — all kinds of it. In this chapter we will focus on clarifying just what is meant by networking, and two important ways to get in touch with those who know about job openings: telemarketing firms and job fairs.

NETWORKING

Networking can be defined as developing and keeping relationships with others. Networking involves staying connected to people to keep track of such things as new ideas, services, advancements, and, of course, job openings. Networking is most successful when done consistently over time. When it works, networking can "net" many gains for you personally and in your job search in particular. We will discuss several aspects of networking: how to go about it, sample questions to use when talking to people about positions, and some do's and don'ts of networking.

"But I don't really know anyone; how can I network?" This is a common concern among those who realize the importance of networking but really aren't sure how to go about it. Everyone knows someone, and that someone knows someone else. Just as computers are now linked to one another to share information, people have always been connected in some way. The most obvious people who would have a prominent place in your network would be your immediate family members. Next come your friends, associates, schoolmates, professional people such as doctors or lawyers, member of associations to which you belong, or maybe even the coach of your son or daughter's soccer team!

You must consider everyone you meet as a potential contact. The person who cuts your hair, the counter person at the deli or coffee shop, everyone! To help you explore just how many individuals you really do have in your network, fill in the following Network Planning Sheet, and remember you are naming people who may have direct access to positions and people who are in your life who know other people, who know others, who know ....

Network Planning Sheet

Use this list to identify people who will become your first level of contact. It can be an effective starting point for your expanding network of people.

List Family Members

Parents _____

In-laws _____

Sisters _____

Brothers _____

Others _____

Contacts from Previous/Current Jobs

Employers _____

Co-workers _____

Customers _____

Clients _____

Competitors _____

Others _____

Contacts from School

Administrators _____

Professors/teachers _____

Alumni _____

Classmates _____

Sorority/fraternity members _____

Others _____

Contacts from Worship/Church

Clergy _____

Church leaders/officers _____

Religion teachers _____

Ushers _____

Others _____

Contacts from Leisure Activities/Hobbies

Club members _____

Card/game groups _____

Physical fitness club members _____

Sports team members _____

Others _____

Network Planning Sheet (continued)

Contacts from Having Children

School administrators _____

Teachers _____

Parents of child's friends/classmates _____

Parents in carpool _____

School coaches _____

PTA/PTO _____

Parents in school-sponsored groups (Boy, Girl Scouts, etc.) _____

Others _____

People I Know from the Past

Neighbours _____

Friends _____

Customers/clients _____

Former Employees _____

Others _____

People I Know from Public Service/Charitable Organizations

Community Fund _____

Chamber of Commerce _____

Local government groups/committees _____

Environmental groups _____

Public safety groups _____

Jaycees/Rotary _____

Other volunteer groups _____

Professional People I Know Who Know a Lot More People

Doctors/dentists _____

Accountant _____

Banker/financial advisor _____

Insurance agent _____

Hairdresser/barber _____

Mechanic _____

Other repair personnel _____

Now that you've determined names of people to include in your potential network, devise a plan or schedule for contacting these people. Spread the word now!

Where and how can you do this? As you are sitting in the barber's chair, the accountant's office, or the grade school auditorium during the Christmas program, strike up a conversation with some of these people about your job search. Sometimes opportunities to network come up in idle conversation. Let's say your hairdresser asks you about your plans after college graduation or the parent of your child's playmate asks you what line of work you are in. These can be perfect opportunities to develop conversation and at the appropriate time include a statement about your current career goals. Examples of such statements are as follows:

Hairdresser:
> "Well, Bill, what are you planning to do after graduation in June?"

Job seeker:
> "After graduation, I hope to become a programmer in a mainframe environment. Do you know any programmers or anyone seeking to hire programmers, or who use the services of programmers?" or "Do you know anyone who is involved in the computer industry?"

Father of son's friend:
> "So, what do you do when you're not coaching T-Ball?"

Job seeker:
> "Currently, I am in sales of basic electronics. But I'm planning to make a career move and am interested in telecommunications. What line of work are you in?"

Father:
> "Actually, I work in the cellular communications industry. We're a pretty big operation."

Job seeker:
> "Really? What is your company? Who is the Human Resource Director there?"

In addition to bringing up your career goals in casual conversation, you can be more direct. A physician, a sister-in-law, or a minister may already be aware that you are looking for employment. Therefore, in these circumstances all you need to do is initiate a conversation. If you wish, instead of asking about anyone who is hiring, you could always see if your potential contact has any acquaintances who are in that or a related industry or who have other direct or indirect contacts.

For example, your dog's groomer may have another client who has a sister who works for a software company. Or, you may have an uncle who serves on the village water commission with a woman whose daughter works in a major insurance firm that employs programmers. The key here is to "spread the word." Ask questions, strike up conversations, ask your contacts if they know of other potential contacts. This type of personal networking is efficient and effective! Try it!

Some suggestions concerning conversations to have with potential contacts include some basic questions to have in mind in any networking circumstance, and some ideas for questions to ask of people whom you don't know but who have been referred to you by others.

Basic Questions to Ask Referrals
- Do you know anybody who might have or know of a job opening in my field?
- Do you know anybody who might know someone who would?
- Do you know or can you refer me to someone who knows a lot of people?

Basic Questions to Ask a Contact Who You Don't Know
- How did you obtain your position or get into this field?
- What do you like (or dislike) the most about your job?
- Do you have any suggestions on how a person with my qualifications and skills might find a job in this field?
- What trends do you see in this field or how does the future look in this field?

DO'S AND DON'TS OF NETWORKING

Finally, here are some of the Do's and Don'ts of Networking from the book *Networking,* by Mary Scott Welch.

1. Do try to give as much as you get from your network.
2. Do report back to anyone who ever gives you a lead.
3. Do follow up on any leads and/or names you have been given.
4. Do be businesslike in your approach.
5. Do keep in touch with your old network as you grow.
6. Do call members of your network for no reason at all.
7. Do continue to expand your network.
8. Do be clear about what you are looking for.
9. Do include all ages of people in your network.
10. Don't be afraid to ask for the help that you need.
11. Don't expect your network to function as a placement office.
12. Don't be discouraged if someone brushes you off.
13. Don't be shy; speak out and be assertive.
14. Don't pass up any opportunities to network.

In summary, consider everyone you know or meet as potential contacts. Look for things you have in common with that person. Develop and use a short career goal statement that you can easily share with people. It's probably also a good idea to carry extra résumés with you. You never know when they may prove handy to have. Keep some spares in your briefcase or in the car! And remember, **almost 75 percent of all positions are found through networking**. It can be hard work, but it does pay off.

TELEMARKETING

We've already discussed why networking is so important in your job search. We've also made some suggestions for whom to include in your network and how to contact these individuals. Later in the chapter, we talk about another useful way to spread the word about your job search: career fairs. It is important to realize that a major vehicle for networking and followup to career fairs is using the telephone. Indeed the telephone is an integral part of a successful job search.

USE OF THE TELEPHONE

How many ways can you think of that the telephone could be used in your job search? For what purposes could you telephone someone? List your ideas below.

_____

_____

_____

_____

_____

_____

If you gave yourself some time to reflect on this question, you saw that there are many ways that the telephone can and should be used for a job search. Among these are to perform your networking, to seek information, to answer a classified ad, to follow up on a mailed résumé, to follow up on an interview, to contact references, to follow up on leads received from contacts, to thank contacts, to thank references, and to call family and friends to tell them that you got a job! As you can see, there are many ways that the phone can be used. Specific advantages to using the phone include:

1. You can contact many employers in a short amount of time.
2. You can get information faster and easier than with conventional mail.
3. You are more likely to be able to contact the person doing the hiring.
4. You will know what to expect or be more comfortable when it's time for the interview.
5. You will be able to communicate your personality; you'll be more than just a name on a résumé or a signature on a letter.
6. You can save money and time (and none of us has enough of these!).

TELEPHONE TECHNIQUES

Now that we've seen the advantages of telemarketing yourself, you may be asking yourself, "Just how do I call people? What do I say? What if someone hangs up on me?" These are very good questions. Keep in mind that calling a potential employer not only saves you time, but also gets people's attention. Because of this, and because everyone is busy (including you) and does not want to waste time on the phone, you need to list the companies you want to contact, plan your calls, write down at least the key points of what you want to say, practise, and be willing to follow up and follow through.

List Companies

Before you let your fingers do the walking, you will want to do your homework. Make a list of the companies or places where you would like to work. Ask people you know for suggestions and phone numbers; use the Yellow Pages and other reference books or directories.

Plan Your Calls

Good planning pays off when using the telephone. When do you think is the best time to try to reach business people? 8:00 a.m.? 12:30 p.m.? 5:00 p.m.? Truthfully, the old rules of not calling at the beginning, middle or end of the day don't always apply anymore. In this era of people working nontraditional or flexible hours, many people have rather unusual work schedules. However, you can still try to stay away from the first hour or so of the workday. Would you want any job seekers calling you at that time? The midday may not be an effective time to call either. Again, with varying hours, people may be taking lunch anytime between about 11 a.m. and 2 p.m. So when is the best time to call? Probably around 10:00 a.m. or maybe 3:00 p.m. If that isn't always convenient for you, go ahead and call during those other times. It's still a lot better than not calling at all. You may also want to be careful about calling on Mondays and Fridays if you can at all avoid it. In conclusion, probably the very worst time to call would be at 8:00 a.m. on a Monday or 5:00 p.m. on a Friday! However, there are some who feel that calling very early or late may just find the hiring authority at his or her desk working alone.

Write Down What You Want to Say

When making an important phone call, you don't want to forget anything important, and you want to be as confident as you can. Therefore, it may be a good idea for you to write down what you want to say. Some believe that a script is appropriate; others feel that just the key points that you want to make are necessary. It doesn't really matter: do what's most comfortable for you. However, if you do use a script don't read it word for word or make it sound memorized. Figure out what you want to say to this employer and what details are the most important. The employer will probably want to know three things about you right away: Who are you? Why are you calling? What can you do for me? Outline your answers to these and any other related questions. Remember, you have a very short time to get your message across.

Practise

Before you make your first real calls, practise. After you have completed your script or outline, speak the ideas out loud in complete sentences. Listen to your words and how your voice sounds. Do you sound professional and confident? Next, practise with a friend. Give him or her a call and role play the various characters of job seeker and employer. Ask for feedback and adjust your message, if necessary. You may even want to audiotape yourself to see how you actually sound over the phone.

Follow Up and Follow Through

If you are fortunate enough to make connections or arrangements with someone you have contacted, be sure to confirm the appointment as it draws near (this follow up could be done for something like an informational interview or a visit to the company). If you have had the unhappy experience of reaching message machines or voice mail, be patient. Call back again at a different time. Don't bother to leave a message; you want to speak to people directly. If you keep getting a person's secretary, keep trying as well. And always be courteous to receptionists, secretaries, and assistants. These people often decide who gets to talk to their bosses and who doesn't!

Calling strangers cold or without some type of referral can be a very scary prospect. How do I ask for the person I need to talk to? Here are some examples of how you might initiate contact:

_____ Could I speak to the person in charge of your Communications Department?
_____ I would like to speak to the supervisor of your field technicians.
_____ Could I please speak to the manager of your Engineering Department?
_____ I am interested in speaking to the person in charge of your Public Relations Department. Who would that be?

You may also want to try calling a company and telling the person on the phone that you have some correspondence to send to the head of the communications department, engineering department, etc. (This would not be untrue since you would like to send your résumé to that person.) Ask for that person's full name and full address. Then wait a few minutes and call back and ask for that person by name.

If you get a secretary when you call, and that person asks you what your call is in regard to, you can always say you need to discuss some correspondence (résumé) or you need to talk to his or her boss about an appointment (interview). You may even say that you have a business matter to discuss. Whatever you think you might like to say, don't ever consider saying that it is personal or that it is a personal call. That's dishonest and won't get you anywhere.

One last tip regarding your telephone requests, when you do reach the hiring authority, you introduce yourself and he or she is listening to you, it's best not to ask for a job interview but rather for an appointment. If you are requesting an informational interview or another type of personal meeting, let him or her know that you want only 15 or 20 minutes of time. If your contact is considering seeing you, you may want to try the sales technique of asking if a Tuesday or a Wednesday is better. Before or after lunch? When busy people are asked questions like these, they often respond automatically (e.g., "Wednesday is better" or "Before lunch is more convenient"). Then you are on your way to finalizing a meeting.

Finally, remember this list of Do's and Don'ts for successful use of the telephone in your job search.

TELEPHONE DO'S

— Prepare yourself before calling

— Practise telephoning with a friend

— Set up a daily plan

— Keep pen and paper handy for notes

— Keep a log of your activities

— Turn around objections

— Keep a smile on your face

— Time your call carefully

TELEPHONE DON'TS

— Drink a beverage, chew gum, or smoke

— Allow background distractions or noises

— Sound as if you're reading a script

— Speak too softly

— Talk too technically

— Rush through your presentation

— Interrupt your contact

— Act as if your contact can't see you

— Be overbearing

— Leave a message

The following is a sample script which can be studied and used to get the feel of how a telephone conversation might go.

SAMPLE SCRIPT

CALLING THE HIRING MANAGER

Switchboard: "Acorn Cellular. May I direct your call?"
Caller: *"Yes, could you please tell me who hires the field service engineers at Acorn Cellular?"*

Switchboard: "I believe that is Mrs. Creighton in Personnel."
Caller: *"I'd rather speak to someone in the field service department. Do you know who the manager is?"*

Switchboard: "Well, that would be Mr. Kinsie."
Caller: *"May I please speak to Mr. Kinsie?"*

Switchboard: "Yes, one moment and I'll connect you."
Mr. Kinsie: "Field Service Department. This is John Kinsie."
Caller: *"Good afternoon, Mr. Kinsie. My name is Carol Curtis and I'm very interested in employment at Acorn Cellular and was wondering if you were in need of an experienced field engineer."*

Mr. Kinsie: "Well, I really don't have any openings at this time. Are you representing someone?"
Caller: *"No, I'm looking for that kind of work myself. Do you anticipate any future openings?"*

Mr. Kinsie: "There's a possibility we might be promoting some of our Field Service staff in a few months. At that time we might be interested in speaking with someone like you. Why don't you send a résumé to my attention, and I'll take a look at your qualifications."
Caller: *"Thank you very much, Mr. Kinsie, I will get my résumé in the mail right away. Again, my name is Carol Curtis and I really appreciate your time on the phone today."*

Mr. Kinsie: "Sure, no problem. I'll expect your résumé in the mail."

MEETING OBJECTIONS ON THE PHONE

One sure thing about calling business people for information or appointments you will meet objections. It's natural. Try not to be discouraged by them, and try to be persistent without being obnoxious. A useful goal could be to try to get at least one thing from each call you make. Perhaps it's some information, another contact, or an interview. Whatever the goal is, you need to remember a very useful communication technique for meeting objections. In his book *Guerilla Tactics in the Job Market,* Tom Jackson details a three-part technique for dealing with objections. He states that the majority of people when confronted during a phone call with an objection from another person, oftentimes stop in their tracks, apologize, and back off or even hang up. That is what you feel like doing, but don't do it. Instead, use the following three-part technique which is a key element in successful interpersonal communications.

How to Handle an Objection

Step 1: Get It: Don't pretend you didn't hear it or that it is untrue.
Don't argue about the objection.
Allow the person on the other end of the line to experience and know that you did receive the objection.

Step 2: Respond to It with a Benefit or Value: Try to respond with a statement of benefit that can overcome the objection without denying it. Let the other person know that although you heard, understand and grant the truth of the objection, you still have something of value to offer that will benefit the listener.

Step 3: Reintroduce the Original Request: Repeat your original statement or request that drew the objection in the beginning.

Below are some examples of how this technique might work.

You: Would it be possible for us to meet next week?
Contact: *I don't think so. You don't have the kind of experience we are looking for.*
You: Yes. That's probably right (**Step 1**). However, I think that the experience I do have could be very valuable to you in several ways (**Step 2**). If we could talk for 20 minutes, I could demonstrate what I mean, and how I feel I could contribute to your department. Could I have 20 minutes of your time next Tuesday or Wednesday? (**Step 3**).

You: I would like to stop by and discuss this with you further.
Contact: *Well, I can't talk to you today. I'm going out of town on a sales trip.*
You: Yes, I know you must be very busy (**Step 1**). However, if you could find a few minutes to meet with me when you return, I think I can help your staff with sales incentives and motivational techniques (**Step 2**). Please tell me when you will be returning so we could discuss this further (**Step 3**).

Two very important parts of this process are to make sure that you let the listener know that you heard the objection (**Step 1**), and to respond with a benefit or value (**Step 2**). Don't overlook either step.

PREPARING YOURSELF TO MEET OBJECTIONS

Here are some objections that can be heard when asking for a meeting with an employer. Write our your answers to them, and make sure you include all three steps necessary for meeting an objection successfully.

Contact: *I'm sorry, but we only interview candidates with at least two years' experience on the job.*

You: Step 1:

Step 2:

Step 3:

Contact: *Well, we might be interested in considering you, but there's no need at this point for an interview. Just send us a résumé in the mail, and we'll let you know when we're interviewing.*

You: Step 1:

Step 2:

Step 3:

Contact: *We won't be hiring until after our fiscal year ends. Why not contact us in three months?*

You: Step 1:

Step 2:

Step 3:

Contact: *I'm afraid we have recently cut the size of our department by nearly one-third. There's really not much point.*

You: Step 1:

Step 2:

Step 3:

Contact: *You say you have ten years of experience in this industry? Frankly, I don't think we could afford someone with those qualifications.*

You: Step 1:

Step 2:

Step 3:

CAREER FAIRS

Career fairs are excellent ways to meet and greet a large number of potential employers at one time. Career fairs are usually formal gatherings of recruiters held at area hotels or large meeting facilities. Typically, career fairs include many recruiters who have immediate openings to fill as well as some recruiters who are there to publicize their companies and gather résumés for future openings. Regardless, career fair attendance is useful for any job seeker. Why? It gives you an opportunity to network personally and pass out as many copies of your résumé as you can. It also provides a chance to improve social communication or interviewing skills. At the same time, you may even meet other job seekers at a career fair who can become potential contacts for you.

The Basics

Career fairs are usually advertised in the classified advertisement section of major newspapers or through mailings. Some ask a small admission fee, while most are free. Career fairs usually run from morning to night, allowing for both the unemployed and currently employed to attend. Some fairs are most specific and designed for job seekers in a certain discipline such as engineering or medicine or sales. Also, some fair organizers will advertise their events for people with some experience rather than recent college graduates, who usually meet recruiters on their campuses. In any event, consider attending several fairs.

Some career fairs are not for the faint of heart. You must be willing to walk up to a booth and stick out your hand and introduce yourself. You must be able to give a concise career statement and be able to talk to the recruiter about the company and the position. You must also be able to answer questions about skills and qualification: and articulate your goals. And you must be willing to compete with a possibly huge crowd of people who are trying to do the same thing! Here is a sample career fair conversation for someone looking for employment:

Sample Conversations

Candidate: "How do you do? I'm John Sutton. I'm happy to see a representative from Collin Systems here."

Recruiter: *"Pleased to meet you, Mr. Sutton. Are you interested in our telecommunications coordinator position?"*

Candidate: "Yes I am! I am currently employed as a LAN administrator and am looking for greater challenge in a new position. Here's my résumé. You'll see I have a related degree and five solid years of experience in this field. I'm very interested in hearing more about your opening."

This discussion gives you an idea of how easy it can be to approach a recruiter at a career fair. Be friendly, be natural, and be direct.

The following sample conversation is one that could take place when a potential candidate, let's say a student, is attending a career fair to make contacts or get information rather than seeking an immediate position.

Student: "Hello, Mrs. Norausky, my name is Taylor Lawrence. Although I won't be graduating from college until June, I am interested in learning about career opportunities in hotel/motel management. Can you tell me about your organization?"

Recruiter: *"Why, certainly. Highsmith Incorporated is an international firm which owns hotels in 10 major cities across the United States and Canada. We are always interested in competent people trained in hospitality management. If you would like, you may take some of the literature on our organization that I have here."*

Student: "Would you mind if I took one of your business cards in case I have a question later on?"

Recruiter: *"Help yourself. Good luck with your future career, Taylor."*

CAREER FAIR TIPS

Even though career fairs may seem intimidating to some, remember, employers are there to meet you. That's why they came. Put on your best suit, smile, and get ready to start selling yourself! The following are some final tips on career fair attendance.

- Come dressed as you would for an interview (clothes, shoes, hair, jewellery).

- Take along plenty of résumés for distribution and a supply of business cards if you have them.

- Take a pen and portfolio for notetaking and collecting materials.

- Find out in advance which employers will be at the fair and know something about the ones in which you are particularly interested.

- Talk to every employer about direct openings or for networking opportunities.

- Approach employers individually, not in groups.

- Take advantage of lull times or times that are less crowded; for example, 12 noon or 5:30 p.m.

- Look the recruiter in the eye and use a firm handshake.

- Prepare a brief presentation of career goals, background, and skills and accomplishments to use during the fair.

- Be prepared for a possible on-the-spot interview.

- Have some insightful questions in mind to ask the recruiter.

- Work hard at maintaining your energy and enthusiasm.

- Take short breaks but don't break your momentum.

■ Follow up within a week with a letter to each recruiter you met. Include the following:
  — A thank you for information and time
  — A review of one or two of your primary qualifications with a reference to your knowledge of the company
  — A request for an interview and a statement that you will follow up the letter with a phone call within a week or two

QUESTIONS

1. What is the most effective means for acquiring job leads?

2. Who should you consider as potential contacts for your network?

3. Give examples of two of the basic questions to ask a contact who you don't know.

4. What are some advantages to using the phone in your job search?

5. What suggestions are given in this chapter on planning your telephone calls?

6. What are the three parts to Jackson's technique for meeting objections on the phone?

7. Give three advantages of career fair attendance.

8. What are some potential lull times for career fair activity?

9. What can be included in a followup letter written after meeting a recruiter at a career fair?

1. Using the network planning sheets found on pp. 83 and 84, make a list of 5 to 10 types of contact that you feel would be your best bet. Why did you select these particular contacts?

2. Create a sample conversation in which you ask a networking contact to review your résumé.

3. You have found an interesting career fair publicized in the Sunday paper. You are a bit uncomfortable about going to the fair alone, so you arrange to go with four of your good friends or classmates who are also looking for jobs similar to the one you want. You know you will feel much better going up to strangers with some of your friends around you. Is this a good idea? Why or why not?

After completing this chapter, you will:

Understand the types and forms of interviews.

Be familiar with the general structure and format of a typical interview.

Effectively prepare yourself for interview questions.

Develop proof stories to use in interviews.

Consider type of questions to ask during interviews.

Understand the basics of negotiating.

Consider using informational interviewing to your advantage.

9 THE INTERVIEW:

The Ultimate Business Meeting

Next to the résumé, the interview is the most important tool in your job search toolbox. The résumé is necessary to let people know who you are and assist you in setting up an interview. However, the interview is the key to employment. During an interview, you have the opportunity to personally present your qualifications and experience to an interviewer. More important, though, is the interviewer's assessment of your personality, interpersonal and communication skills, and ability to fit into the organization. A recruiter is not just interested in a list of your courses, your degree, or other résumé items. A prospective employer wants a qualified employee who is a team player, is able to communicate, can take advantage of opportunities, has a high energy level, keeps an upbeat attitude, and demonstrates high ethical standards. The interview is the most important business meeting you will ever have.

This chapter covers information on the following:

- ■ Types of Interviews
- ■ The Basics
- ■ Preparing for the Interview
- ■ Interview Questions
- ■ Proof Stories
- ■ Questions You Can Ask
- ■ Traits Employers Seek
- ■ Negotiating Salary and Benefits
- ■ Professional Portfolio
- ■ Information Interviews

TYPES OF INTERVIEWS

Interviews may be one of several types and take one of several forms. By knowing what you may encounter, you'll be able to determine the nature of and prepare properly for any interview. The three basic types of interviews are:
— Referral interview
— Screening interview
— Selection interview

*A **referral interview*** gives the employer a look at you for future reference. This could be as a result of networking, common contacts, etc. Sometimes a referral interview may open the door to a job opportunity before it is advertised. In any case, a referral interview can put you in touch with valuable contacts.

The purpose of a **screening interview** is for an employer to narrow the field of applicants. The interviewer reviews your qualifications to find reasons to reject you, and may check your résumé for inconsistencies. When this type of interview is granted, it is often conducted by human resource personnel. Your best approach during a screening interview is to follow the interviewer's lead. Keep your responses concise, but remember, this may be the only chance you have to sell yourself.

Those who come through the screening interview usually go on to a **selection interview**. In this type of interview, a supervisor or department head will try to determine from your answers, past experience, and attitudes whether you're right for the job. By noting how you listen, think, and express yourself, the interviewer can decide whether you are likely to get along with others in the organization. This interview process usually ends in a hiring decision. Your best approach during a selection interview is to show interest in the job, relate your training and experience to the company's needs, listen attentively, and display enthusiasm.

FORMS OF INTERVIEWS

Interviews may take one of three basic forms:
— Directed
— Unstructured
— Stress

The **directed interview**, generally used in the screening interview, is highly organized from start to finish. Often working from a checklist, the recruiter may ask a series of prepared questions within a specific time period. Your answers are noted in writing. It is interesting to note that some directed interviewing may be done over the telephone.

In contrast, the less formal **unstructured interview** has an open and relaxed feel. By posing broad questions, the interviewer encourages you to talk (sometimes causing you to divulge more than you should). Used in selection interview situations, this form of interviewing provides you with an opportunity to bring out your unique personality and to demonstrate that you are the best person for the position.

The unstructured form is often used in combination with the **stress interview**. This approach intentionally puts you under stress so that your reactions are observed. For the unsuspecting applicant, the experience can be unsettling. Stress interviews may consist of pointed questions designed to cause you to have difficulty in responding. The best way to handle this form of interview is to remain calm and try to concisely, but accurately, answer questions put to you. A stress interview may be conducted by one person or several people.

INTERVIEWING: THE BASICS

Now that we've discussed the types and forms that interviews can take, let's take a look at more particulars of interviewing. No one can say how long an interview will take. Certainly a very short interview is not a good sign; conversely, a longer interview is more promising. Interviews can last from 15 minutes to the major part of the day if they are conducted by several people. It really becomes several shorter interviews but may feel like one huge one! For discussion purposes, let's take a look at a 30-minute interview. The figure below shows the breakdown of time and the phases of a typical 30-minute interview.

30-Minute Interview

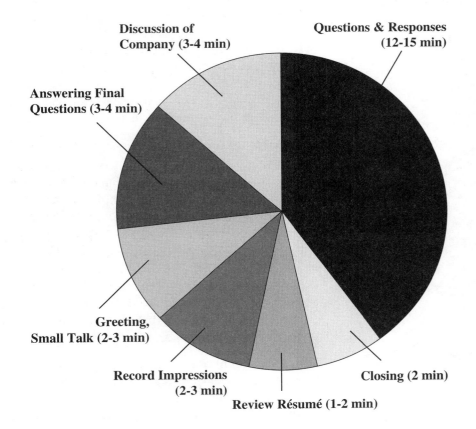

Discussion of Company (3-4 min)

Questions & Responses (12-15 min)

Answering Final Questions (3-4 min)

Greeting, Small Talk (2-3 min)

Record Impressions (2-3 min)

Review Résumé (1-2 min)

Closing (2 min)

Résumé Review

These few minutes are taken for the interviewer to refresh himself or herself about you by scanning your résumé. Be keenly aware of what you have said about yourself on your résumé. During this phase of the interview, or possibly later during the business phase, the interviewer may ask you questions on key information found in the résumé. In any event, it may take several minutes to reread your résumé. This quiet time can be a bit unsettling to you: avoid the temptation to start justifying or clarifying anything on your résumé. Just wait for any questions or for the next phase of the interview to begin.

Greeting, Small Talk

Realize that this phase and the previous one may be switched from the order that you see here. Whenever it does happen, the greeting and small talk portion of an interview are designed to put both you and the interviewer at ease. The greeting is usually accompanied by a handshake. (This handshake can occur before the résumé review phase.) When shaking the interviewer's hand remember not to offer too weak or too strong a handshake. A firm meeting of the hands with one or two shakes is appropriate. By custom, the interviewer should extend his or her hand first. If this doesn't happen you have two choices: extend your hand or continue with a verbal greeting. Do whatever makes you feel most comfortable.

As you can see in the visual on the previous page, the small talk phase is rather brief. The interviewer may ask about your trip to the facility, comment on the weather or make another comment. Follow the interviewer's lead. Talk casually and politely, making a positive first impression. Sometimes hiring authorities may be uncomfortable in the interviewer role and may wish to continue the small talk indefinitely. This is rare, but if it does happen, you may want to advance the conversation into the next phase by saying something about the company or position.

Discussion of the Company

Either before or after the question and answer session may come a few minutes' discussion of the company by the interviewer. He or she may tell you a bit about the company's history, mission, current markets, departments, and future goals. You should already have discovered most of this information through researching the company. Listen to the comments and ask questions for clarification. As part of your company research keep informed of companies that are being discussed in the media. If this firm has recently been mentioned in stories or coverage in the media, you may want to mention what you heard, that it impressed you, and you may want to ask further questions. This can be very complimentary to the interviewer as long as you stick to positive media coverage about the company.

Getting Down to Business: Questions and Responses

This is the real meat and potatoes part of the interview. This is when the most information is exchanged and first impressions give way to an overall impression of the candidate. The first thing to realize about questioning in an interview is that it is not a one-way street. Make sure that all your questions on the company and the position are addressed as well by the end of this phase. There are fairly typical questions which are asked at this point; they may include the following:

— Tell me something about yourself.
— Describe your strengths.
— Describe your weaknesses.
— Tell me your qualifications for this position.
— Why should I hire you?
— What can you contribute to this firm?

Take each question as it comes and respond fully and accurately. Sometimes it is appropriate to ask a question to clarify what is wanted in an answer. For example, when you are asked to tell something about yourself, what do you say? Where do you start? Does the interviewer want to know about you personally or professionally? You may want to say, "What would you like to know?" or "Where would you like me to begin?" If the interviewer doesn't care, you decide what would be appropriate to mention at this time. A tip is to begin with some recent achievement or qualification, rather than where you attended primary school!

This portion of the interview tends to have a rhythm of its own. Questions and answers may come at a fairly consistent pace. Don't be shy about asking your own questions. Later in this chapter, there will be samples of questions you may be asked as well as questions that you may want to consider asking. If you don't understand a particular question or if you have forgotten the latter part of a multipart question, do ask to have the questions explained or repeated. Also, do not bring up any questions on salary or benefits in early interviews. This should be reserved for later. At the end of this chapter you will read more about negotiating in an interview.

Answering Questions from the Applicant

There is usually a time near the end of the interview when the rhythm has slowed, most information has been covered, and things wind down to closure. Commonly, the interviewer will ask the candidate if he or she has any questions. Think carefully before responding. Go over in your mind all the issues and information that has been covered. See if there is anything that remains unclear to you. Don't be afraid to ask. Intelligent questions never seem silly or stupid. If, for some reason, you think of a question or two after you have left the interview, that's all right. You will be sending a follow-up letter, and that is a most appropriate place to ask questions that didn't come to mind during the interview itself.

Closing, the Next Step

After all questions and answers have been covered, you're finished. The interview has ended for all practical purposes. At this time, the interviewer may thank you for coming in or use another phrase that signals that the interview is through. As an active job seeker, you need to know what the next step will be in this interview process and when it will occur. If the interviewer doesn't mention the next step, you need to ask. You could ask when you might hear from the interviewer, or if he or she has many interviews to complete before a decision is made on further interviewing or selection of an employee. You could also ask for the interviewer's card and ask if it is OK for you to call in a week or so if you have not heard from him or her. You need to remember that you want to leave the interview either with a strong idea from the interviewer of when you will hear something, or by making sure the interviewer knows you will be following up with a phone call. Knowing time frames and next steps in the interviewing process helps you to balance the requirements of this interview experience with others you are having at the same time. A firm understanding of what the next step will be and when it will occur also prevents you from sitting and waiting for the telephone to ring!

It is extremely important at this point to make sure that the interviewer is aware of your interest in the position. Make sure you thank them and restate your interest before leaving.

PREPARING FOR THE INTERVIEW

Writing Down Impressions

This is the time the interviewer will spend recording his or her impressions of you. If you were introduced and had discussions with others in the company, they will contribute their impressions of you as well. There's not much you can do now about this phase except to ensure that when you walked away from the interview, you left with a firm handshake and a warm smile.

Now that we have taken a look at the phases of the interview, let's go over more important aspects of interviewing. Like anything else that you want to become successful in, interviewing requires planning and preparation. Review the following list to help you prepare for a successful interview.

1. **Remember to find out as much as possible about the company.**
   This includes the type of work they do, their financial situation, who their competitors are, how employees feel about working there, etc. Review the chapter on researching companies if necessary, for more specifics.

2. **Find out as much as you can about the position.**
   If you have applied for it, you already know the basics, but try to find out more. Call the Human Resources Department and tell them you will be interviewing for a certain position. Ask them to give you a further description of the job and its requirements. After you have a good view of the position, relate your own background and abilities to it point by point in your own mind. This comparison will be quite useful later on in the interview itself.

3. **Practise reviewing your strengths, skills, accomplishments.**
   Talk about yourself to yourself out loud and then to a friend. Listen to yourself talking about your experiences and how they relate to the job. Think about comments you may wish to add or delete at this time.

4. **Be aware of typical interview questions and practise your answers.**
   Lists of interview questions appear later in this chapter. Study them and rehearse your responses out loud. Keep in mind how you want to answer these, but don't try to memorize any answers.

5. **Prepare a list of questions for the employer to answer.**
   You can either keep these in mind or write them down. What do you need to know to be able to make the best employment decision for you? Samples of these questions are found later.

6. **Have an idea of what the competitive salary is for the position and know your own salary requirements.**
   Sometimes it is not easy to learn about salaries. If you cannot get information on a particular position in a firm, at least have an idea of what the going rate is for someone who would have the amount of training and experience necessary to fill the position. Professional associations, professional periodicals, and other resources can be helpful for this information.

7. Collect any information you think you may need for the interview.

In a briefcase or portfolio, assemble items that may be useful in the interview process. These could include extra copies of your résumé, letters of recommendation, a list of references, work samples, well written documents, etc.

8. Select and prepare the proper clothing.

The interviewing culture is still fairly conservative. A conservative suit in conservative colours is appropriate for both men and women. Make sure clothing is well pressed and maintained. Make sure shoes are polished and jewellery is kept to a tasteful minimum. You don't want anything in your appearance to speak louder than you.

9. Prepare mentally and use the power of positive visualization.

To lower your stress and to help you relax later during the actual interview, mentally rehearse the entire interview as it might happen. Visualize yourself dressed and ready to go. See yourself walking in and shaking hands confidently. Picture yourself seated and answering questions clearly and impressively. Visualize yourself as a comfortable, relaxed, and successful candidate!

More tips on preparing for the interview include details on the company, the process, and the follow up. After you have researched a company and are preparing to interview with a representative from it, there may be some data you would like to get on the company that was unavailable in your company research sources. You may want to consider asking about this information during the interview. Basically, you should already know the company's correct name, location, products or services, number of employees, and how long the company has been in business. The list below includes some additional topics of interest. You may wish to select some of these for your own purposes.

You May Want to Ask About...

___ Potential growth for the industry or firm

___ Potential new markets, products, services

___ Organizational structure and philosophy

___ Management style(s)

___ Number of plants, offices, and locations

___ Type and extent of training

___ Relocation policies

___ Typical career paths, advancement philosophy

___ Use of technology, types of equipment

Before discussing interview questions, here are some other final interview tips covering the procedure itself and the follow up.

— Don't chew gum or smoke.

— Thank the receptionist or secretary for making the appointment or for assistance.

— Listen for names when introduced. Speak to the interviewer by name when appropriate but don't be so bold as to use first names.

— Make sure you get a business card or precise spelling of names for follow up. You may always call the Human Resources Department later for these if necessary.

— Remember that not all interviewers are good at it. They also may feel nervous or uncomfortable. Try to establish rapport but don't let their nervousness affect you.

— Decide how you want to handle inappropriate questions if they should come up. Later in the chapter is a list of questions employers should not ask you.

— Decide if you want to take notes during the interview. If you think you would like to write a few things down, ask permission first. Then make sure you are not more involved in notetaking than interviewing. Keeping good eye contact is essential.

— Try to speak the jargon of the position or industry. Use enough industry language to show you know what you are talking about, but avoid any temptation to throw too much jargon around.

— Remember to send a short follow up letter after the interview. Also, send a letter to anyone else with whom you may have had a substantial conversation. It is courteous to thank your references for their kind words and use of their names as well.

Finally, reflect on past interviews in an effort to learn your interviewing strengths and weaknesses. You may want to ask yourself some of the following:

— What in our conversation most interested or impressed the interviewer?

— Did I present my qualifications and traits well? Did I forget any?

— Did I miss any opportunities to market myself?

— Did I make sure I learned all I need to know about the position and company?

— Did I talk too little or too much?

— Was I too aggressive? Tense? Shy? Uncertain?

— How can I best improve my next interview?

After you have evaluated yourself with questions like these, think of tangible ways to make your next interview as good or better!

INTERVIEW QUESTIONS

In this section we will present typical interview questions. Let's start with the most common questions asked by interviewers. These include the following:

— Tell me about yourself.

— What are your strengths? Weaknesses?

— Why should I hire you?

— What are your long- and short-term goals?

In addition to these questions, here are more you may want to think about. Some of these relate to career or job experiences and expectations and some are more personal in nature.

— Why did you choose the career you are in, or which you are preparing for?

— What are the most important rewards you want from your career?

— Tell me about your work experience. How do you think a friend would describe you?

— What motivates you to put forth your greatest effort?

— What have you learned from your mistakes?

— What accomplishments have given you the most satisfaction?

— How have you demonstrated your ability to contribute to a team effort?

— Give me an example of how you have solved a problem.

— Give me an example of when you have performed successfully under stress.

— If you were to write a description of the ideal position for you, how would it read?

— What do you like/dislike about your present position?

Of course these are just a handful of questions; there are many more that may come up during an interview. Using the following worksheet pages, practise creating answers to some more interview questions.

Interview Question Worksheet

How would you describe yourself?

_____

_____

How would your current/past supervisor describe you?

_____

_____

What are some of the activities you particularly like to do on a job?

_____

_____

What are some activities you prefer to avoid on the job?

_____

_____

What are your short-term goals?

_____

_____

Why are you leaving your current job? (for the currently employed)

_____

_____

What is your current grade point average; do you feel that it is a true reflection of your knowledge and ability? (for the student or recent graduate)

_____

_____

(continued)

Interview Question Worksheet (continued)

What goals did you set for yourself in the past year, and which ones did you accomplish?

_____

_____

Describe a time when you had to juggle a number of priorities. What was the end result?

_____

_____

Why do you feel you are the best candidate for the position?

_____

_____

What are your strengths?

_____

_____

What do you think it will take to be successful in our company?

_____

_____

What accomplishment has given you the most satisfaction and why?

_____

_____

What motivates you to put forth your greatest effort?

_____

_____

Behavioural Questions

Finally, more and more employers are now using what are called *behaviour-based* questions in interviews. This type of questioning revolves around the candidate revealing knowledge, skills, and abilities in answers to specific situational-type questions. These are structured patterns of questions designed to probe past behaviour in situations similar to those encountered in the job that is open. A candidate responds to questions with examples from past situations. Responses to these questions tell the interviewer something about the candidate's specific reactions to past circumstances. This can supply the interviewer with a more complete profile of the candidate and his or her behaviours than traditional interview questions can.

Often these questions can reveal various traits, skills, or behavioural areas to the interviewer. Some of the areas for which questions can be asked include communicating with others, supervision, analyzing data, dealing with change, self-management, team building, etc. Here are some examples of behaviour-based questions:

— Tell us about a difficult situation you have dealt with in supervising others. What was done and what were the results?

— Tell me about a time when you had to collect, manipulate, and/or analyze data.

— Describe a time when you had to use your finest oral communications skills. What was the circumstance and what was the outcome?

— Describe a time you took an idea or concept and turned it into a program or project.

— Describe a time when you had to adjust to change. How did you cope or adjust to this change?

— Explain your role as a group/team member.

— We all face disappointments in life. Tell me about a time when you had to handle disappointment or rejection.

— Give me an example of a time on the job when you showed initiative.

— Tell me about a time when someone made an unreasonable request of you. How did you react and what happened?

— Describe a time when you were most frustrated or discouraged in reaching your objectives or goals. How did it turn out?

— Describe the last time you did something which went well beyond the expected in work or school.

— Tell me about the most difficult challenge/problem you've faced and how you handled it.

PROVE YOUR TRAITS WITH PROOF STORIES

A very effective technique for dealing with all kinds of interview questions, including behaviour-based questions, is the telling of a story or stories in an interview. Before you think we're talking about fictional storytelling, we're not. What we are talking about here is a way to impress interviewers by telling a story that helps to prove the qualities that you say you have. This is a way for job hunters to prove what they've said about themselves on their résumés is really true.

Think about it for a moment. What do most of us like to hear and tend to remember? Stories. Stories are specific, entertaining, and often memorable. And isn't that what we are looking for in our interviews? We want the interviewer to remember us and our qualifications. And stories are memorable, so stories have their place in the interview.

Consider this scenario: A campus interviewer has just completed a day of talking to 15 graduating seniors. All graduates have the same degree, similar qualifications and even similar grade point averages. But one student, Karen, is remembered more than the others. In response to discussions of job qualifications, most students said they were dependable, flexible, and were good problem solvers. Karen also mentioned these traits needed for the job, but in addition she told brief stories that proved or verified what she was saying about herself. Let's call these proof stories.

Proof stories help you demonstrate specific skills that you possess and that the employer will be impressed by. These skills can be technical in nature (the ability to program in a specific computer language) or they can demonstrate transferable skills (the ability to work independently). Whatever traits or skills you use them for, they are *proven effective*.

HOW TO CREATE A PROOF STORY

Let's take a look at how to create a proof story. A proof story takes only a few minutes to tell, relates directly to traits sought for the position, and has three distinct parts to it. To develop these stories you must first review actions and activities of your past and develop a list of key traits that you possess. Some of these traits can be those related on your résumé, personal strengths and skills, and typical traits you know that are needed for the type of work you seek.

Once you have developed a healthy list of traits, reflect on situations and circumstances wherein you relied on those traits or skills. For example, if you say you work well under pressure, you could use as your proof story an incident when you successfully worked a double shift during the holiday season. Another example could be a story showing that you used good communication and problem-solving skills in solving a computer-user's problem over the telephone. Get the idea? Remember, interviewers are more likely to listen to and recall specific stories about specific incidents. Therefore, instead of trying to tell a story by saying that you work at a hospital emergency room and almost always work under pressure, think of a specific evening or time when things were extremely hectic or challenging and tell about that.

Now that you have a basic understanding of proof stories, use the following worksheet to help you develop some of your own.

Proof Story Worksheet

List below some technical, personal, and transferable skills or traits which would be useful for proof stories.

_____

_____

_____

_____

Use the following format to set up your own proof stories.

Trait or characteristic this story demonstrates _____

1. **Set up the background to the story.** Briefly describe the situation that called for you to use the skill. Where were you? What led to the situation?

_____

_____

_____

_____

2. **Describe the action that was taken or the response that was given.** Based on the situation above, what happened? What did you do? When and where did you do it? How and why did you do it? This description should contain action verbs that help create a powerful story.

_____

_____

_____

_____

(continued)

Proof Story Worksheet (continued)

3. **Reveal the results that occurred due to the action taken.** What was the end result? Try to quantify results whenever possible or measure what happened against a standard. Don't hesitate to brag about the results achieved: that's the purpose of the entire proof story!

_____

_____

_____

_____

In relating this story, you may have discovered that it displayed other traits. List them below.

_____

_____

Some key points to remember when creating proof stories:

— Try to have several stories in mind when you begin interviewing.

— Don't go into extensive detail in the background section. Reveal just enough detail so the listener can understand the basic story.

— Don't lump your results statements in with your action discussion. Clearly describe the actions taken. Then create transition to the last part of the story, the results.

— Try to create a story that reflects one specific incident or setting. Stories that are too broad lose impact.

— When you finish your results statements, link the ending of your story back to the trait mentioned at the beginning.

— Use these stories to discuss how you meet various requirements of the job. After you have gotten the interviewer to describe the ideal candidate for the position, prove to him or her that you are the one with the aid of your proof story.

— Keep stories in mind and use a couple during your interview, but don't overuse them.

SAMPLE PROOF STORIES

Here are some sample stories to read to get a feel for level of detail and concreteness necessary for these stories to work well for you.

Characteristics this story demonstrates: *clear thinking, leadership skills*

1. One evening when I was the supervisor in charge at a major furniture warehouse, our sprinkler system malfunctioned and water began soaking all our stock. The sprinklers had been operating for 10 minutes, so we had to move fast to salvage the inventory.

2. I got on the intercom system and alerted all personnel in the front warehouse area and in the break room. I arranged the workers in teams and gave them various responsibilities to fire up the lift trucks, move the stock to unaffected areas, and clean up the affected area.

3. Within three hours, $880 000 worth of furniture had been moved to dry areas and saved from severe water damage. Warehouse facilities were cleaned and stock was returned to normal storage areas within five hours. The entire staff felt a sense of pride and accomplishment in their efforts.

Other characteristics from this story include working well under stress, dedication.

Characteristic this story demonstrates: *customer relation skills*

1. I was working as a field service technician for a major electronics company. My job was to troubleshoot and repair electronic copy machines and mail machines. One day I was dispatched to a law firm where the copy machine had been experiencing numerous problems. When I arrived, the office manager met me at the door and started shouting about the lack of reliability of our equipment. He also said that he needed to get important documents copied within the hour or there would be serious ramifications.

2. I listened patiently to the manager describe his situation. I probed with questions on the nature of the problem and how long it had been occurring. I immediately ran some diagnostics but was still uncertain as to the problem. With the manager huddling over my shoulder. I removed the back panel to discover a broken program switch which was causing the problem with the machine. I assured the office manager that the equipment would be up and running within the hour.

3. After thirty minutes, the copier was operational. Although the copier was no longer under warranty, I did not charge the customer for the part as a goodwill gesture. The office manager was impressed with my speedy repair, grateful for the break, and managed to get his important document copied in time.

Additional characteristics from this story include good communication skills, working well under pressure.

INTERVIEW QUESTIONS YOU CAN ASK

Not only is it important for you to answer questions well and provide proof stories whenever possible in an interview, but it is also important for you to ask pertinent questions. Remember when we said that interviews should be dialogues? It is very important that you probe and get answers to questions that will assist you in making sound employment decisions. One of the best ways to learn as much as you can about a company, position, or circumstance is to ask questions, questions designed specifically to get to what you need to know. Let's divide these questions into three categories:

— General

— Defining

— Controlling

General questions are asked to gain useful information for later decision-making. These questions could include the following:

1. If I am hired, will there be a formal training program or on-the-job training?
2. What are the expectations for new employees?
3. Is there a probationary period? How long is it?
4. How is an employee evaluated and promoted?
5. If I am hired, who will be my immediate supervisor? Can you tell me about his/her management style?
6. What are the opportunities for personal growth in your company?
7. Describe a typical assignment that I might receive.
8. What will I be doing on a daily basis? What particular things will characterize my day?
9. How much travel is normally expected with this position?
10. What characteristics does a successful person have in your company?

Defining questions to ask interviewers help to define hiring criteria, allow interviewers the opportunity to brag about their company, and help to set up proof stories for you. Some defining questions would include the following:

1. What are your objectives for this position? What would you like to see accomplished by the person filling this position?
2. How does this position fit into the overall objectives or goals of your company?
3. What are the organization's (or department's) principal challenges? Opportunities?
4. What are you looking for this department/position to accomplish in the next year or so?
5. What principal skills are you looking for in the person selected for this position? What key technical, educational, or personal traits do you desire?

Controlling questions to ask interviewers are a little trickier than either of the above types. They are trickier because they are designed to seek answers to sometimes difficult but necessary questions. When used effectively, controlling questions can help you avoid accepting a position with a company where you might be unhappy or unsuccessful. Although there is no guarantee that these questions will achieve this, they certainly are useful in getting at some important issues. Because of their potentially negative nature, controlling questions should be used selectively and sparingly. They should be tried only after there is a mutual conclusion that you are qualified for the job, and you have demonstrated a sincere interest in the position. Some of these types of questions may even be used after an offer has been made.

1. Why is this position currently open? What happened to the incumbent? How long has it been open?
2. If the incumbent is still in the company's employment, what is he or she doing? Is this a typical career path for this position?
3. What resources (budget, personnel) and authority go with the position? Does this position include hiring authority?
4. What type of chain of command exists with this position? Who must approve my actions or decisions?
5. In the past, what has been your organization's response to economic down-trends?
6. What is the company's policy toward tuition assistance?
7. What are the strengths and weaknesses of this company?
8. What management style do personnel in this company employ?

Interviewing can be a hectic but exciting time. Prepare for it, anticipate some setbacks, and try to relax and enjoy it too. Realize that there are some questions that are considered unlawful to ask during a job interview. These questions relate to your age, your marital status, whether you have children and their ages, your physical conditions beyond what is necessary to perform the job, your arrest record, your religious affiliation. Remember, these are things that are typically inappropriate to be asked in an interview. However, you may find these or similar questions on some application forms.

TWELVE TRAITS EMPLOYERS SEEK

Before we discuss some final comments in this chapter on negotiating, the College Placement Council has named twelve traits that it feels employers frequently seek in candidates. See how many you have and what ones you may be able to successfully communicate to your potential employers.

1. **Ability to communicate**
   Do you have the ability to organize your thoughts and ideas and present them effectively? Can you express yourself clearly in speaking and writing? Can you present your ideas to others in a persuasive way?

2. **Intelligence**
   Do you have the ability to understand the job? Can you learn the details and contribute original ideas?

3. **Self confidence**
   Do you demonstrate a sense of maturity that enables you to deal positively and effectively with people and situations?

4. **Willingness to accept responsibility**
   Are you a person who can recognize what needs to be done and is willing to do it?

5. **Leadership**
   Can you guide and direct others to meet recognized objectives?

6. **Energy level**

   Do you have a forcefulness and capacity to make things move ahead? Can you maintain consistent enthusiasm for your work?

7. **Imagination**

   Can you confront and deal with problems that may not have standard or easily recognizable solutions?

8. **Flexibility**

   Are you receptive to new situations and ideas and are you capable of change?

9. **Leadership skills**

   Can you bring out the best efforts of individuals and teams so that they become effective and efficient?

10. **Ability to handle conflict**

    Can you successfully contend with stressful and antagonistic situations and people?

11. **Competitiveness**

    Do you have the capacity to compete with others and be measured by your comparative performance?

12. **Goal achievement**

    Do you have the ability to identify and work toward specific goals? Are you willing to work toward goals which challenge your abilities?

NEGOTIATING SALARY AND BENEFITS

These comments on negotiating are probably more appropriate for individuals who have been in their field for some time and have professional experience and accomplishment with which to barter. A word of caution to recent college graduates who do not have business or industry experience: don't try it. Successful negotiating requires a proven track record with a previous full-time position, a past salary history, an appreciation of typical job benefits which can be offered, and an idea of the net value you have in the marketplace.

The Issue of Money

For any job seeker, however, the issue of money is an important one. Keep in mind that you want to sell your skills for the highest price or salary possible, and your potential employer probably wants to purchase your skills at a somewhat lower price. Remember, when the issue of money comes up, you should try to postpone it to a later time. Salary really isn't an appropriate topic for the beginning of a first interview; you haven't decided if this is the position for you and the interviewer doesn't know yet if he or she is interested in employing you at all let alone for how much money. Keep in mind **whoever talks about money first loses.** If it's the employer, you have a high card to play in the negotiating game. If it's you, you may have to mention an amount or salary range that is either too high (deadly) or too low (again, deadly)! Keep in mind that when you are in the interview, you want to stress that you want to be a part of the firm so you can make a significant contribution to the company, the department, and the person interviewing you. Let the interviewer bring up salary first.

If and when you are asked about your salary requirements, you should respond with a phrase like this: "Although salary is an important consideration, my primary interest is getting a career opportunity which benefits the company and gives me challenge and growth at the same time." If the interviewer becomes insistent about salary requirements, try asking "What is the salary range for the position?" Again, this deflects the mention of numbers back to him or her. If a range that is acceptable to you is mentioned then you can tell the interviewer that this is in your range.

One important point to remember is that you must determine your lowest acceptable salary before you get into a negotiating situation. If you do this, you can be more confident negotiating for a job you may really want. Remember, a difference of a thousand dollars or two becomes negligible after it's divided by 24 pay periods and taxes and benefit payments are taken out! In addition, with careful planning and successful work performance, you may be at a more desirable salary level within the first year or so.

The Benefits Factor

There is one more option you may have in this salary game. That is the possibility of negotiating benefits. In addition to any possible bonus situation, you may be able to discuss additional funds for professional and personal development, extra vacation or insurance, and other options. Remember, these items should become an issue if there is an offer that you feel is somewhat below your established market value. If you try this kind of negotiating when a fair offer of salary has been made, it just may backfire!

Below are some examples of items that may be used for negotiating benefits. You must first see if the company you are interested in offers many of these for the position you are discussing.

Sample Benefits Which May Be Negotiated

Athletic club membership	Housing
Bonuses	Legal assistance
Children's scholarships	Loans or loan guarantees
Company car, gas allowance	Matching investment programs
Compensatory time	Pension plan
Consumer product discounts	Profit sharing
Cost of living increases	Relocation expenses
Country club membership	Retirement plan
CPA or tax assistance	Sales commission
Day care	Stock options
Deferred compensation	Travel
Dental plan	Vacation
Disability pay	Vacation discounts
Educational fees	Wholesale buying
Flexible work hours	

PROFESSIONAL PORTFOLIO

As a job candidate today, you need all the ammunition you can get to succeed in your job search. An important tool to have in your arsenal is the professional portfolio. This tool contains samples of your finest work, whether taken from academic experiences and assignments or from previous work experiences and projects.

The use of portfolios is becoming more widespread by savvy job candidates. They realize that employers are very interested in seeing first-hand how and how well candidates can demonstrate their skills and perform their work. Tangible examples are useful weapons. The portfolio is an extremely effective tool in helping to achieve this goal of proving yourself. Once you have a good portfolio prepared, you will find you have numerous opportunities to use it in the interview process. Now that we've talked about the importance of the portfolio, let's take a look at what types of materials are suitable for this collection.

Materials to Include

Depending on your specific skills and competencies, there are many types of sample materials which can be included in the portfolio. As part of this portfolio preparation process, write down the most prominent skills you have, both technical and nontechnical, and consider a variety of documents and examples that can demonstrate these specific skills. For example, if you are looking to demonstrate computer programming skills, you may select a particularly challenging program you have written or debugged. In addition to samples of specific skills or competencies, you will want to include some or all of the following typical samples. Below are definitions of typical samples followed by suggested samples to include arranged in two categories: portfolio samples for new graduates and portfolio samples for experienced individuals.

Table of Contents: Use this depending on the length of your portfolio. Remember you can also set up your portfolio to either include or exclude information depending on the position you are applying for.

Goals: You need to be careful here. This area could really be a useful addition provided you word it to succeed within the company you are applying to. Never indicate a goal is to operate your own business, even as a long term goal.

Ethics Statement: A paragraph or two about your general work ethics and values can assist you in selling yourself. Don't forget to back this up with examples or further details.

Résumé: An impressive résumé demonstrates good career planning and self-knowledge. It can help prove to an employer that you have the best background, education, and experience for the job.

Photographs: These may include pictures of you receiving awards, of you in publications, or a shot of an event you planned. Photos should be good quality and placed in a plastic sleeve.

Computer Disks: Electronic means can be used to store a variety of material: writing, data, and graphics .... nowadays it can also include multimedia! Materials to be placed on disk can range from computer programs, to accounting procedures, to formal proposals you have written.

Writing Samples: Samples include term papers, articles that have been published, business correspondence, recommendation reports, feasibility reports, etc.

Letters of Reference, Commendation: Reference letters include those from current and past employers proving your ability to perform in the workplace. Commendation letters could be congratulatory letters received for winning awards, receiving academic honours or performing well on a job. You may also wish to include customer letters of commendation.

Employer Evaluations: These can be written when you successfully complete an internship or possibly a cooperative education assignment. Some evaluations from other part-time, summer, or volunteer work may also work here.

Performance Reviews: Depending in the size and format of this instrument, you may want to share the entire document, or the summary page or comments.

News Articles: If a paper has included a piece on your job, awards or honours received, save a copy to include.

Certificates of Completion: These can demonstrate completion of professional workshops, seminars, etc. You can demonstrate a desire to remain up-to-date in knowledge and skills by displaying these documents.

Grades, Transcripts: Demonstrating achievement in both technical and nontechnical coursework can be useful. Generally, grade reports and transcripts are offered in portfolios to show above-average and outstanding course achievements.

Program Information, Course Outlines: If you are a recent graduate include relevant course outlines or program details. These may be available from your college/university calendar. Some institutions provide program competencies.

Manuals, Procedures Developed: A procedural manual you have developed or contributed to on your job or for a club or organization is a good sample of several capabilities.

Samples for New Graduates	Samples for Experienced Individuals
Résumé	Résumé
Photographs	Photographs
Computer disks	Computer disks
Writing samples	Writing samples
Letters of reference, commendation	Letters of reference, commendation
Employer evaluations	Performance reviews
News articles	News articles
Certificates of completion	Certificates of completion
Grades, transcripts	Manuals, procedures developed
Program, course outlines	

Arrangement of Materials

Now that we've viewed some suggestions of samples to be included in portfolios, how should they be put together? To develop a portfolio with impact, review all pieces you are thinking of including. You can arrange pieces chronologically or thematically according to skills demonstrated. You will want to consider jazzing up your presentation with colour, graphics, and unique but tasteful title pages.

Types of Portfolios

This is up to you and the profession you are in or hope to enter. If you must display large artwork, you will need to visit a special art supply store. If you will display traditionally sized materials (81/2 x 11 inches), you can use a three-ring binder, a plastic folder, or perhaps a notebook with tabs. Presentation is extremely important. Think about the message you are trying to convey. A leather (or look-alike) binder with materials protected in plastic sleeves will sell you more than a plastic binder and pages three-hole punched. Pay attention to the smallest detail when you are putting your portfolio together. The potential employer will be sure to notice these things. A note of caution: after you have assembled and packaged your portfolio, try to have duplicate copies of items for which you are unwilling to leave the originals. Always have duplicate copies of everything, just in case.

Presenting Your Portfolio

As soon as comfortable in an interview discussion, mention that you have brought some materials or samples of your work for review. Wait until you approach the question-and-answer portion of the interview before referring to materials in the portfolio. Use it to illustrate the application of skills you are promoting. Don't try to use the portfolio to answer questions about your qualifications or skills. First describe what you have done or can do, and then demonstrate it with samples from your portfolio.

Last, to create a memorable final impression of yourself, present a "leave-behind" piece from your portfolio to the interviewer. This can leave a lasting impression of you long after you are gone.

INFORMATIONAL INTERVIEWING

A discussion of interviewing would not be complete without a mention of informational interviewing. Informational interviewing is just what the name implies: interviewing for information only, not for a job. This is an excellent way to learn about companies and typical positions, to develop contacts for later job seeking, or to get some advice from someone on such topics as résumés and interviewing. Also it can serve as practise to develop conversational skills, skills that are a necessary part of the job search. Informational interviewing is a way to open doors and learn about opportunities firsthand. But in this type of interview, you are seeking advice, guidance, and information only.

Informational interviews should take place before you begin your job search interviews. Try aiming fairly high in an organization for informational interviews. Call the company, ask for the proper department or individual. Talk to the employer about setting up a mutually convenient time for a talk. Although this is not a job search interview, dress as if it were one. Make sure you do some research on the company as well so you will be able to have a knowledgeable conversation. Also, bring along a professional-looking résumé (for your contact to comment on) and a list of questions that you want to ask. At the close of the informational interview, as you thank the person for his or her time, ask the contact to suggest one or two other people with whom you might be able to speak. Follow up the interview with a brief, but formal thank-you letter.

Here are some typical questions that you might find useful for informational interviewing. These questions are appropriate when speaking to someone in a career similar to the one you wish to pursue.

1. Can you describe a typical day in your position?

2. What do you like best or least about your job?

3. What steps did you take to gain this position?

4. What are the most prominent skills used in this position?

5. What is a typical career path for someone in your job?

6. What is your work environment like in terms of pressure? Deadlines? Routine assignments and activities?

7. If you could, what are some things you would change about your job or the company?

8. Can you refer me to someone else who can provide me with further information?

QUESTIONS

REVIEW QUESTIONS

1. What is the difference between a referral interview and a selection interview?

2. Which segment of the interview usually takes the longest?

3. As you get ready for the interview, what type of information should you prepare?

4. What are behavioural interview questions?

5. What are proof stories?

6. What are the three parts of a proof story?

7. What are the differences between general, defining, and controlling questions that you can ask during an interview?

8. What was one piece of advice from the chapter on negotiating the issue of money?

9. What is a professional portfolio, and how can it assist you in the interview?

10. What are informational interviews, and when should they take place?

DISCUSSION QUESTIONS

1. What are some of the challenges of stress interviews, particularly the ones where you may be interviewed by more than one person at a time?

2. Give examples of the proper dress for a male and/or female about to go on a professional job interview. Don't forget to talk about personal grooming and shoes too!

3. When you meet the recruiter for the first time, there often will be a handshake. Who should extend his or her hand first? What type of grip is best? What conclusions do we sometimes draw by the way in which someone shakes our hand?

4. Create an answer for the questions "Tell me about your strengths. Tell me about your weaknesses." Do you think humour should ever be used when dealing with questions like these? Why or why not?

5. Write a proof story for one of your most prominent traits. Share these in class and have classmates suggest additional traits that your story may suggest.

6. Review the 12 traits that employers seek on pages 114 and 115. In your opinion, which one or two are the most important and desirable?

CHAPTER
OBJECTIVES

After completing this chapter, you will:

Be familiar with types of job search testing.

Understand the purpose of testing.

Be able to approach testing circumstances knowledgeably.

10 TESTING:

A Job Search Reality

Tests are used for many different reasons by employers. Some use them as screening tools to help limit the number of candidates they need to interview. Employers go to a substantial amount of trouble and expense to administer tests to candidates. Why? They use tests as tools to assist them in hiring the best people possible technically, intellectually, emotionally, ethically, and physically. Testing may be inevitable in your job search. Don't let it worry you. There are really no ways to prepare for these tests. All you can do is make sure you understand why a test is being administered, the conditions under which the test will be given, and the directions for taking the test. If you know about the testing ahead of time, try to get a good night's sleep and try to be as relaxed as possible when taking a test.

TYPES OF TESTS

What types of tests can you expect in your job search? It is not possible to predict the exact tests you may take; however, here is a list of the most typical tests that job seekers have reported taking.

- **Aptitude tests**: These can be tests of your general knowledge in such areas as word analogies, verbal comprehension, abstract reasoning, mathematics, and number and letter series. Included in this category would be any **technical aptitude tests** given to assess technical or subject area competencies.

- **Personality tests**: On occasion, some psychological testing is done by companies. These tests usually have the candidate react to a variety of questions or scenarios designed to categorize the candidate with certain characteristics or behavioural types.

- **Drug tests**: The most popular type of substance abuse testing used by companies, these are physical tests which are used to determine the amount of substance or chemicals in the body. (More details on this trend in testing later.)

These tests can be administered in several different ways. A general aptitude test is often a pencil and paper type test (or a computerized test). A technical aptitude test can also be pencil and paper or verbal (such as technical questions asked during an interview). Personality tests are usually pencil and paper type tests; however, some candidates have reported having interviews with company psychologists to determine personality types and related behaviours. Drug tests are physical exam-type tests. Because it is relatively inexpensive, the urinalysis is the most common type of drug test. This test may be given separately or as part of a general physical exam.

TIPS ON TAKING TESTS

Now that you have an overview of what tests you might be taking, here are a few tips about subjecting yourself to testing. Keep in mind that no one can force you to take any type of test. You have the right to refuse a test; however, if you do, you may expect the interview process to end or be severely curtailed. If you do agree to testing, ask to delay testing until after the interview. If you are successful with this request, you can avoid the test being used as purely a screening tool. This way, the interviewer will be able to assess you as a person rather than just a test score. Remember, if you ask to postpone a test, assure the interviewer that you are willing to be tested but would like a chance to discuss the position and your qualifications before a test is given.

Before taking a test ask how it will be scored, or how the results will be measured. Will incorrect answers be subtracted from correct ones? Is there any penalty for guessing? It is a timed test? Are unanswered questions marked wrong? Also, make sure you are given a quiet, distraction-free environment for test taking.

For pencil and paper tests, keep a few basic rules of test taking in mind:

— Read the directions carefully before starting.

— If you are unsure of an answer, skip it and return to it later.

— For timed tests, make sure you are aware of how much time has passed.

— Read questions deliberately; misread questions (or directions) can be disastrous.

— Keep in mind when taking a test that your first answer is usually the correct one. Change test answers only when you are sure that it is necessary.

Some Thoughts on Drug Testing

Because employers want to make sure that they employ individuals who will contribute to the company's productivity and profit, they do not want to hire people with substance abuse problems. Employees with serious substance abuse problems may have more accidents, take more time off, and may file more health insurance claims. Employers cannot afford these increased costs or the associated risks. Therefore, substance abuse testing, particularly drug testing, has become a permanent part of the employment scene. Drug testing is becoming more common in business and industry for existing employees as well as potential employees. Chances are you may have to take a drug test. A mentioned before, urine tests are the most common type of drug tests. You will be asked to give a urine sample.

Before you give a urine sample, make sure you have reported any prescription drugs you may be taking. It is also a good idea to mention any over-the-counter drugs that may be in your system as well. In addition, many people are not aware of the retention time many drugs have in the body. Alcohol may have a retention time of up to 12 hours, while traces of marijuana can exist in the system for up to five days. Be aware that reluctance to take a drug test probably will severely hurt your chances of employment and may destroy your chances altogether. All testing, including drug testing, is serious business to employers. Be prudent and realize that something as important as your job and your future should be protected. It's important that every job seeker realize how serious employers are about maintaining a drug-free environment.

In conclusion, try to maintain a positive attitude about the testing that is part of your job search. Whether you face aptitude, personality, drug tests, or all three: You have faced tests before in your past school and training, and you probably did fine. Remember that testing is just one more hurdle you need to clear before you get the perfect job for you.

QUESTIONS

REVIEW QUESTIONS

1. What are the three types of test discussed in this chapter?

2. Why is it recommended that you try to postpone a test until after the interview?

3. Why has drug testing become a permanent part of the employment scene?

DISCUSSION QUESTIONS

1. Do you think you can prepare for an aptitude test?

2. Do you think you should ask for a copy of written test results?

3. What are some techniques you may want to employ to place yourself in the best possible environment and frame of mind for taking written employment tests?

11 JOB SEARCHING ON THE INTERNET:

The Electronic Edge

This chapter is a separate detailed discussion of using the Internet in your job search. Why? Because anyone wishing to compete for positions now and as we move into the new millennium MUST be familiar with and comfortable using a variety of electronic means, particularly the Internet.

How Do I Get the Electronic Edge?

If you do not have your own computer or access to the Internet, many public libraries, local universities, and community colleges offer both the equipment and the training to use the Internet. Take a quick course or ask a knowledgeable friend to help you. If you were ever considering getting a computer and/or signing up for your own Internet access, this is an excellent time to do so. The computer is an invaluable tool for a variety of aspects of your job search, and an Internet account offers opportunities to explore and use this awesome network to your advantage.

What's In It for Me?

Having access to the Internet gives you the ability to use, among other things, e-mail and the World Wide Web. E-mail is an almost instantaneous means of communicating with someone through a written-memo format. The World Wide Web is a large part of the Internet wherein such items as company home pages, information on job searching, and contact with companies that can post your résumé exist for your information. There are special search engines (internal software programs that are quite easy to use) that can guide you through researching any imaginable topic on the Web... job related or not!

The discussion in this chapter assumes that the reader has a basic knowledge of the Internet. If you don't have this knowledge, seek out a friend to help you, take a quick course, or visit your local bookstore and purchase a book on the Internet. You may also find useful information in magazine and newspaper articles at your local library. Ask the reference librarian to help you learn the basics of the Internet. Many libraries and commercial video rental stores even have videotapes you can check out on the Internet. The Internet truly is the electronic advantage for anyone seeking information and communication in this age or technology. *(Refer to the Internet Primer on page 131.)*

USEFULNESS OF THE INTERNET

Just exactly how can the Internet be used in your job search? There are a multitude of ways including, but not limited to, the following:

- **Position Openings:** Sites exist which display classified ads from newspapers across the nation as well as opportunities abroad. Corporate home pages often list open positions and ways to apply, sometimes right over the Internet. In addition, commercial job search sites include their own job banks of employers and positions.

- **Résumés**: There seems to be limitless material on the Internet concerning résumés. You can get assistance in writing them, post them with professional agencies, and even include one in your own home page.

- **Researching Companies**: More and more firms are establishing their presence on the Internet. Learning about companies from information they post on the Web is essential and quick. Many sites include the history of the firm, a listing of its products and services, and even e-mail addresses of its employees. Other, more objective sites, can give you statistical and factual information on firms.

- **Networking**: It may seem strange to think you can network over the Internet. but you can! The Internet provides a new level of access to the hidden job market and individuals who can help you tap into it. Three techniques used to network on the Internet are corporate home pages, virtual job fairs, and Web-based forums or discussion groups that can be found through Usenet or Chat options.

- **Professional Job Search Sites**: There are many firms that exist for the sole purpose of helping individuals with their job searches. Some of these agencies and companies help for free; many will assist for a fee. The Internet sites for these companies range from those posting job listings, to some that assist with résumé writing and interviewing techniques, to others that provide general job hunting advice and resources. Consider as many of these sources as possible but be sure you know what you are getting before you agree to pay for anything.

- **Publication of More Traditional Job Search Materials, College and University Sources**: Companies that used to publish job search resources in printed volumes are making their materials available electronically on the Internet. Publishers of such sources as Peterson's Guides and publishers of books on the job search are including materials from their publications on the Internet. Publishers' home pages (such at Prentice Hall's at www.phcanada.com) may also be good sites. Also, you may be able to find useful materials through home pages of colleges and universities throughout the nation and the world. Many career services or placement departments are making materials available to their students and general audiences through postings on the Internet.

You may find additional resources on the Internet through using search engines. You can even find some useful ideas or information by chance as you are using sources from some of the categories above. Sometimes an individual's home page can even be useful as sources or gateways to even more information or sources. Get the idea? The possibilities are limitless!

A Note of Caution

The list of job and career resources on the Internet grows every day. It can be exciting, exhilarating, amusing, confusing, exhausting. In any event, it can be time consuming and perhaps addictive. A note of caution is probably good to give you at this point. It might be best to think of the Internet as a huge library that gives you access to materials and services from a wide range of sources. Evaluate those sources. Do they have a history of producing accurate and trustworthy information? Evaluate the services. Are they designed to help you? Are there fees involved? You may find that many sources and service agencies fit your needs, but you simply don't have the time to read and/or use them all. Be selective, and use your time wisely.

SITES FOR NEW COLLEGE GRADUATES

So How About a List of Some Sites?

Before we look at specific sources, it is useful for you to review page 79. Listed on this page are some of the most popular Internet sources, including Monster Board, Career Mosaic, and Campus Work Link. Additionally, please reread the Note on that page concerning Internet sites. Entries into and exits from the Internet occur every minute. It's impossible to have a truly up to date list; however, most sites listed here have been fairly stable. This list is not comprehensive. Also remember, listings of sites are for informational purposes only and are not considered endorsements by the author or the publisher.

Campus WorkLink:	*www.campusworklink.com*
Canada Jobs.com:	*www.canadajobs.com*
Canadian Jobs Catalogue:	*www.kenevacorp.mb.ca/index.htm*
Career Edge:	*www.careeredge.org/*
Monster:	*www.monster.ca*
Work Web:	*www.cacee.com/*

JOB LISTING SITES

Career Mosaic Canada:	*canada.careermosaic.com/*
Careers:	*www.careers.org/*
Globe careers:	*globecareers.workopolis.com*
Human Resources Development Canada:	*www.hrdc-drhc.gc.ca*
Job Bus Canada:	*www.jobbus.com*
+ Jobs Canada:	*www.canada.plusjobs.com*
Job Find 2000:	*www.jobfind2000.com*
Jobpostings:	*www.jobpostings.net*
Net Jobs:	*www.netjobs.com/*
Yahoo Canada:	*www.yahoo.ca*

GENERAL JOB HUNTING RESOURCES

Career Hunters:	*www.careerhunters.com*
Career Magazine:	*www.careermag.com/*
Career Talk:	*www.careertalk.com*
e Resumes:	*www.eresumes.com*
Get Wired You're Hired:	*www.wiredhired.com*
Job Hunters Bible:	*www.jobhuntersbible.com*
Job-Hunt.org:	*www.job-hunt.org*
Quintessential Careers:	*www.quintcareers.com*
The Riley Guide:	*www.dbm.com/jobguide*

A NOTE OF CAUTION: If you intend to check out any of the Internet sites mentioned, be aware that locations on the Internet change with some frequency and your attempt may not be successful. Locations mentioned in this chapter are for example only and are not necessarily recommended by the author or publisher.

INTERNET PRIMER

Job seekers of today need to be aware of and familiar with many different methods of seeking employment; this includes job searching on the Internet. In addition to using résumé writing computer software, you should consider using on-line computext activities for a variety of job search tasks; your competition will.

If you are not already familiar with the Internet and the World Wide Web, here are the basics. The **Internet** is a collection of interconnected computer networks that spread around the world. The Internet started as a U.S. Department of Defense project in order to link research, communications, and defense information, but today it has become the famous "information superhighway" accessible to anyone with a computer and a modem.

Like the Internet itself, the **World Wide Web** originated as government-funded technology. Its primary users were scientists and academics wishing to exchange fast-changing scholarly information, and to facilitate joint research by colleagues from various comers of the globe. Today there are probably hundreds of thousands of World Wide Web servers (computers that store and transmit Web documents) that are available to any computer user who has a modem and a telephone line. Many individuals, including those seeking employers and employees, have discovered this lightning-fast telecommunications tool. The growing popularity of the World Wide Web is due in large part to the ease, speed, and relative economy with which information can be accessed. Web information can be particularly interesting because it can handle graphics.

To be able to discuss the use of the Internet as part of your job search, you need to be familiar with a few basic terms.

- **Electronic mail (e-mail)**: Messages sent via electronic computer networks coupled with electronic mail software. An e-mail address consists of a user name and a domain name; e-mail addresses are used to send e-mail messages to the correct people. For example, to send a message to user Bill Hayes at Clark College you might use the address: *Hayes@clark.edu.*

- **Hypertext** refers to electronic document elements that contain programmed links to other documents. These links usually appear as highlighted words or symbols you can click on to travel to another cyberspace destination.

- **Uniform Resource Locators (URLs)**: Every resource or file of information on the Web has a location that consists of the name of the computer system where the file is stored, the directory path to the specific file, and its file name. The combination of the pieces of information about a file's location is called the URL.

- **Home Page**: A Web site oftentimes contains a home page or the starting page that will be displayed when you access the site. Typically, the home page is deliberately designed to be the introduction to the site with links to the various documents stored at the site via hypertext. Home pages are often a colourful combination of text and graphics, and some are extremely creative.

QUESTIONS

1. List three of the six ways in which the Internet is useful in a job search.

2. What is the difference between a hypertext link found in a document and URL?

1. How much of an advantage do you think there is to being familiar with the Internet and using it for your job search? Personally, which of the six ways to use the Internet discussed in this chapter would have the most benefit for you? Why?

2. Can you name some ways in which the ability to use e-mail can be useful in your job search?

3. If you do not have any expertise with the Internet, how do you think you could learn about it in an inexpensive and convenient way?

*After completing this
chapter, you will:*

*Be familiar with typical
ways to set goals for your
search.*

*Be able to develop a
strategic plan for
contacting companies.*

*Use the worksheet to set
weekly, monthly and career
goals.*

12 JOB SEARCH STRATEGIES

Planning is an important key to success in your job search. Now that you have read through much of the advice in this personal job search guide and worked through its activities, what's your plan? Now that you have gained greater self knowledge, developed a professional résumé, selected your references, generated a sample cover letter to accompany your résumé, researched companies using various sources, prepared yourself to attend career fairs, and begun to network as an integral part of your job search, what now? Now that you are aware of the importance of the interview, where do you really start? You have thought about your chances of negotiating and are prepared to face any types of tests you may be given as part of your job search. Now you need a strategy.

GOAL SETTING

Because everyone has different circumstances and previous knowledge, people start their job searches at different places or with different steps. But all of us are ultimately faced with the reality of the search: the almost overwhelming task of beginning the hunt.

Whether you are starting your job search eagerly or hesitantly, be careful to keep your spirits high, don't take rejection ultra-personally, and operate using self-imposed goals and objectives. But why shouldn't you take rejection personally? It is you others are saying they are not interested in. That's kind of personal, isn't it? Well, yes and no. Even though a recruiter may not be able to use someone with your qualifications, it's not a rejection of you as a good, worthy person. Indeed, a recruiter may like you very much but be unable to offer you a position. After you accept that, move on with the knowledge that someone is out there with the right position for you. How do you keep your spirits high? Different tactics are used by different people: some visualize their success, some can shake off disappointments easily and move on, and others get by with help and support from family and friends. Don't be isolated during your search. Share your goals, feelings, and disappointments with others. It helps.

The best way to find that position as quickly and efficiently as possible is to operate your job search with some very definite goals in mind. These goals need to be tangible, measurable, and achievable. Of course, your main goal is to get a job, but what intermediate and short-term goals must you accomplish to get to that final goal of a position? Start out by writing your career goal. It helps to see it in front of you.

Next are your intermediate or monthly goals. These goals may include contacting 20 people within your personal network within the next month, or distributing 40 copies of your résumé through job fairs, personal contacts, and the Internet. Another intermediate goal could be to have a minimum of five informational interviews and ten cold calls completed within a certain time frame. Get the idea? What makes the goal intermediate is its scope and complexity. The activities for an intermediate goal will be possible to achieve in several weeks or perhaps a few months. These goals are a bit more ambitious than your short-term goals.

Short-term goals are very important. These are the daily or weekly objectives that keep your job search on track and propel you to completion of the other goals already discussed. What are some examples of short-term goals? One could be completing your résumé within the week or creating a scannable résumé by week's end. Another weekly goal could be to contact at least five companies, or to set up four or five interviews for a particular week. A week's goal could be to attend three job fairs and two professional association meetings. You decide. But when you do, make sure your goals are realistic yet challenging. It does you no good at all to have as a weekly goal, say, to send out three résumés. It will be a very long time before you accomplish your long-term goal that way!

It may also be helpful to share your goal with someone who can be your support system. Once you tell someone your weekly plan, it becomes much easier to carry out. It is always easier to meet goals if you are accountable to someone other than yourself. Remember, when you are seeking employment your job is to get a job and you must set your goals accordingly.

Using the space below, try writing several of your own goals. Later expand on this sample list, and keep these goals visible so you can see them every day!

Career Goal:

_____

_____

Monthly Goal:

_____

_____

Daily or Weekly Goal:

_____

_____

STRATEGIC PLAN FOR COMPANIES

Another element that will be part of your goal setting is contacting companies. This is critical and deserves specific mention. How many companies should you contact? Five? Ten? Twenty-five? Fifty? The answer to that question is that you should contact as many as humanly possible. The more you advertise, the more likely you are to make the sale. Let's say you have decided to contact 40 companies; how in the world can you do this short of hiring a staff and opening a campaign headquarters? The way to successfully market yourself to as many firms as possible is through a strategic plan. This is how a typical plan works.

You want to contact 30 companies. You don't have time to call each employer on the phone. You don't have time to call 30 or 40 companies. How can you manage? Given a company list of 30, you need to prioritize these companies into your A list, B list and C list, etc. Your A list includes the companies that you *really* want to work for including your all-time dream company —the top one on your A list. Your B list will be the companies that are also very attractive to you, but these firms are not your top 10 or 20. Your C list are companies you would work for, companies you have some interest in, but these are firms you would not want to spend a great amount of time pursuing.

Now let's place our 30 companies in the proper categories or lists. For discussion purposes, your A list includes your top five companies. Your B list includes the next 10 in priority, and your C list includes the last 15. Write the names, addresses, phone, and fax or e-mail numbers down for all your desired companies including the names or position titles of people you can contact, if possible. Take these 30 company entries and place them into three separate lists (A, B, and C).

The A List

Next, think about the most effective ways for you to reach your top companies. Perhaps you will call first for informational interviews or you will contact the recruiters to set up interviews. You will definitely want to follow up any efforts with personal phone calls. You can ask individuals to review your résumé, determine which companies will be involved in career fairs in the near future, talk to hiring authorities about possible current or future openings, send résumés and fill out applications for all, follow up résumés with letters or calls etc. These are your best job prospects and you want to devote as much time and energy as you can to them. List the activities you will do to reach these firms at the top of List A.

The B List

Now let's look at the second list. This one is twice as large as the first list and includes companies that are good prospects but not ones you will pursue with the same intensity as those on the first list. Perhaps you will call, send your résumés to these companies, check to see if these firms will be interviewing in the area soon, and call some of the hiring authorities. For some companies on this list, you may want to follow up your résumé with a quick call to the firm's Human Resources Department.

The C List

Companies on List C are ones you are interested in, but they are ones you will not pursue aggressively at all. These 15 companies will get the least amount of your time and effort. Perhaps you will merely get the names of recruiters and send a personal cover letter and résumé to each. Because most of your time will be spent calling and following up with companies on the first two lists, you may not even follow up on some of your mailings to companies on this list.

As you develop your own personal strategic plan, you will need to select your own particular companies to include (perhaps based on personal contacts, type of industry, location etc.). You will also need to determine the number of companies in total and on each list, and the contact strategies you intend to use (calling, mailing, interviewing). A sample Strategic Plan follows, to remind you of this process and to get you started in developing your own.

If you have not had a lot of experience with the job search, it may be a good idea to start by contacting companies lower down on the list. In this way you will be able to start to anticipate challenges you will encounter. As you go through this process, your confidence will improve and you will be ready to move forward to your top A list.

Today's job searches are challenging. More candidates are competing, often, for fewer jobs. More media are involved in job searches from a newspaper to the Internet. At the same time you are conducting this sophisticated search, you are attending to your usual responsibilities, whether they be finishing college, working a job, or taking care of a family. You MUST have a plan for your search. A well-thought-out job search strategy is not a luxury, it is a necessity!

A List

Contact Strategies

_____

_____

_____

_____

_____

_____

_____

Company 1:

Company 2:

Company 3:

Company 4:

Company 5:

B List

Contact Strategies

_____

_____

_____

_____

_____

_____

_____

Company 1:

Company 2:

Company 3:

Company 4:

Company 5:

Company 6:

Company 7:

Company 8:

Company 9:

Company 10:

C List

Contact Strategies

_____

_____

_____

_____

_____

_____

Company 1:

Company 2:

Company 3:

Company 4:

Company 5:

Company 6:

Company 7:

Company 8:

Company 9:

Company 10:

Company 11:

Company 12:

Company 13:

Company 14:

Company 15:

QUESTIONS

1. What are examples of career, monthly, and weekly goals?

2. Why is having a strategic plan for contacting companies a must?

1. Think about one or two family members or friends who are interested in your welfare. How do you think these individuals can assist you with your goal setting and keeping, and strategic planning?

2. Can you name two or three companies that would be at the top of your A List?

3. Think through a typical day's activities that are a part of your life at this time and how much time each activity takes (i.e., I spend six hours in class, four hours at work, etc.). Now figure the amount of time you might be able to devote to your job search, either in a typical day or week. Multiply that to see how much time you would be giving to your search in one month. Based on our discussion in this book and your knowledge of the job market you intend to enter, is this enough time? If not, try to re-evaluate your current schedule to see where you might be able to make some adjustments to provide more time for your job search. Share this information with classmates, or in a general class discussion.

13 EVALUATING A JOB OFFER:

Company A or Company B?

No matter if you are looking for your first full-time career position or are making a change of jobs, you will probably need to evaluate one or more job offers. What's the best way to do this? As you read this section, you will see that the criteria for evaluating a job are fairly straightforward. What makes evaluating job offers difficult is that you are often comparing two or more offers that are never totally alike. When comparing offers, you need to use your head or reason as much as possible; however, ultimately you may have to use your heart or emotions to help you make that final decision.

Before we take a look at some criteria to consider when evaluating job offers, it might be helpful to examine some common sense but sometimes overlooked facts or realities about work.

FACTS AND REALITIES ABOUT WORK

1. We are all individuals who have our own values and preferences when it comes to our world of work. What's right for one person may not be right for another.

2. A position you choose to accept will to some extent affect your lifestyle and psychological well-being and will affect your quality of life.

3. There is no such thing as a perfect job.

4. The majority of positions today require 40 or more hours of work a week.

5. A large number of your waking hours per week are spent either at work or commuting to and from work.

TYPICAL CRITERIA FOR EVALUATION

With the above realities and facts in mind, let's examine some typical criteria for evaluating jobs. When you really think about it, there are four basic areas which need to be examined when you evaluate a job offer.

- The organization and its personnel
- The scope of the job
- Salary and benefits associated with the job
- The match between the job and your goals

A CLOSER LOOK

Let's take a little closer look at the specifics which require consideration for each of the criteria above.

The organization and its personnel

- Is the company a commutable distance from home?
- Are the physical facilities acceptable?
- Will I have the physical space and tools necessary for the job?
- Is the work environment formal or relaxed?
- Does the organization have a good reputation?
- Am I comfortable with the size of this organization?
- Am I in agreement with the majority of company policies?
- Do people seem to remain with this company for a while?
- Would this position allow me to work as part of a team or individually?
- Do I see myself making friends with people in this company?

The scope of the job

- Does the position offer a variety of duties?
- Would this position provide a challenge?
- What would a typical day be like?
- Would I be using most of my skills and education?
- Does this position require travel? If so, what type and how much?
- What are the normal working hours?
- Would I be happy getting up in the morning and coming to this job?

Salary and benefits

- What is the salary for the job and how does that compare with my needs?
- What are the intangibles that should be considered along with compensation?
- Does the firm offer competitive medical, dental, life, and disability benefits?
- What is the company's profit sharing, pension or retirement plan, and stock offerings?
- What type of miscellaneous benefits come with this package (e.g. tuition reimbursement, day care, bonuses, recreational programs, credit union, flex time, etc.)?

The match between the job and your goals

- ■ Is the opportunity here for me to meet my long-term goals?
- ■ What is the potential for job growth? Lateral movement?
- ■ What is the schedule and criteria for evaluation?
- ■ What type of average pay increase is typical?
- ■ Will I have the opportunity to learn new job skills?
- ■ Does the company encourage continued education?
- ■ Will this position provide an opportunity to meet other professionals in my field?
- ■ Does this company support professional membership?

Hopefully with a closer look, using the questions from the categories above, you will be able to make a well informed decision about which job offer to accept. Finally, here is some advice in the form of a checklist, to consider as you zero in on making that important career decision.

Do I Really Want This Job?

To assist you with this final decision concerning a job offer, read the following and circle the correct responses. When you are finished, pick up the telephone and call that employer with your decision!

My gut tells me:	yes	no		
The industry fit to my career plans is:				
	excellent	good	fair	poor
The salary is:	high	competitive	low	
The benefits are:	good	fair	poor	
The company/industry is:				
	growing	steady	declining	
The management is:	strong	mixed	weak	
My need for a job is:	desperate	average	casual	
My gut tells me:	yes	no		

QUESTIONS

1. What are the four criteria for evaluating a job?

2. Which of the criteria above is most important to you and why?

1. Which do you think is more important in making a difficult decision about which position to accept: your head or your gut?

2. Salary is important to most workers. If you compared salary to the other three criteria for evaluating a job, which one criterion would win as the most important to you? Which would come in second? How about last?

CHAPTER
OBJECTIVES

*After completing this
chapter, you will:*

*Know the basics of fitting
into an organization.*

*Be able to identify and
understand negative job
behaviours.*

*Have familiarity with top
traits that lead to job
success.*

14 DESIGNING JOB SUCCESS

After you have evaluated your job offers and accepted the position you desire, your work should be over, right? Wrong! Although you should be commended for your sophisticated and successful job search and your success in convincing a company you are the best candidate for the job, in some ways a new type of job has just begun. Along with your new career and its set of job responsibilities and tasks, you have an additional challenge. That challenge is making a good impression as a new employee and setting the stage for your ultimate career advancement. Indeed, this is very important work. But what does it involve?

Fitting into an organization and working well with people may take some effort. There is a breaking-in period for anyone in a new position. Even people who have been in previous professional positions may need to earn their wings in a new work environment. Take time to learn the corporate culture. Become familiar with rules, values, behaviours, expectations. Watch others. Notice who is successful and the techniques these people use. Adopt them and make them work for you. Always provide a solid performance in everything you do from a major project to a written memo. Hard work and the right attitude pay off. Learning how to fit in well in an organization is an initial step toward job satisfaction and career development.

WHAT NOT TO DO

According to the Cooperative Education and Career Services Offices of the College of DuPage, there are several qualities that are surefire ways not to impress a new employer. Results from an American survey of Fortune 1000 company officials indicated the following employee traits and attitudes often lead to serious on-the-job difficulties:

Dishonesty and lying — If an employee lacks integrity, most all other qualities are meaningless.

Irresponsibility, goofing off, attending to personal business on company time — One who wastes the company's resources and is unreliable may not be trustworthy.

Arrogance, egotism and excessive aggressiveness — There is nothing redeeming about someone who spends more time bragging or boasting than working, or one who feels he or she deserves special treatment or privileges.

Absenteeism and lateness — If employees are chronically late or absent, most employers will probably feel employees don't deserve to be paid for time they did not work and work they did not do.

Other undesirable traits mentioned in the survey included not following instructions, ignoring company policies, laziness, lack of enthusiasm, making ill-informed decisions, and taking credit for work done by others.

Another view of strategies for job success comes from the publication *DeVry Directions*. In an article entitled "Survival of the Fittest," editors list ten capabilities corporations demand in new employees. Read through the list below and see how many you already have and how many more you may be able to cultivate.

TOP 10 TRAITS

Excellent verbal and written skills

Employers place special emphasis on the ability to communicate clearly to project teammates, corporate leaders, and subordinates.

Ability to turn theory into practise

Higher level thinking is always desirable; however, companies need personnel who can put into practise what they know. Results are important.

Working well in groups

Companies want team players. Most corporations use project teams of professionals often from different areas of expertise. Many employers typically want staff members to be able to work well in teams of four to six people. This team orientation oftentimes requires knowledge and ability to function with those of different ethnic and/or social backgrounds.

Flexibility

Have you ever heard the phrase, "nothing is more constant than change"? Change is constant in most work environments. Rapid advances in technology and customer requirements combine to make constant demands on companies and their employees. Employees must be able to adapt to and use new structures, programs, and procedures. They need to be flexible enough and willing to change as needed.

Problem solving

Critical thinking skills coupled with good communications skills are essential for today's employees. They must be able to recognize, define, and solve work-related problems efficiently and effectively.

Creativity

Going beyond currently accepted models to find breakthrough solutions is highly valued. Realizing that no single answer is best in every circumstance, individuals must have the confidence needed to take risks and try new and different ideas.

Striking a balance

Today's world is full of stresses. How we deal with these stresses helps to determine who we are and what we are. Those who lead lives balanced with outside recreational and social activities are better adjusted and more productive workers.

Time management

Managing time and meeting schedules are important. Competing responsibilities and multiple work tasks can often be challenging. Effective employees are those who handle their responsibilities dependably and in an efficient manner.

Fearlessness

Although employers do not want reckless behaviour in their employees, they do find that breakthrough successes require professionals who are not afraid of failure. Also, employees who do fail must learn from those failures, adapt, and try again.

Commitment

The ability to be committed and dedicated to corporate or group goals is crucial. Loyalty and goal orientation are key traits. Employees possessing these traits are seen as cornerstones of the corporation. These are the individuals who are responsible for the company's establishing long-range success.

As you can see, fitting into a company and achieving long-term success takes knowledge and dedication. In general, most employers indicate that attitude is everything. A positive attitude will be a major benefit in every organization and is the key to job success. These strategies for job success can result in job security, career development, and ultimate personal satisfaction and fulfillment.

QUESTIONS

1. What are the four things mentioned in the chapter that are destined to lead to serious on-the-job difficulties?

2. Give 5 of the 10 traits that employers look for in new employees.

3. What are some of the essentials mentioned for working well in groups?

1. Think about all the ways that communications exist in a company. How much do you think is oral? How much is written? What do you see as major barriers to successful business communications, and how can these barriers be overcome?

2. Can you give an example of when an employee may need to be flexible in his or her job?

POST-ASSESSMENT SURVEY

It is now time to complete your Post-Assessment survey. If these questions look familiar, it's because you answered them at the beginning of the book. Reflecting on what you have read and learned in this book, answer these question as completely as you can. Then compare your answers to those on the Pre-Assessment Survey on page 3. You may be surprised to see how much you have improved on your answers to the Pre-Assessment Survey. You can see that your career plans are in clear focus, and you are equipped to engage in a successful and rewarding job search.

1. How would you describe your ideal job? What type of activities or responsibilities would you like to have? What type of business or industry do you see yourself working in?

2. What are your personal traits or general job experiences that you would highlight as part of your job search strategy?

3. How do you intend to structure your résumé and what action verbs would be primary in describing your experiences and responsibilities?

4. How long should your résumé be and how would you determine what to put in and what to leave out?

5. What are some of the best methods to research potential employers? What types of information would be useful to learn?

6. What is your personal strategy for marketing yourself to employers? What media would you use? How will you let employers know who you are and that you are available? Where will you go to look for positions?

7. What types of questions will you probably be asked during interviews? What types of questions should you ask during interviews?

8. What techniques will you use to market yourself during interviews?

9. Do you think you will have to take any tests as part of your career search? How will you prepare for these tests?

10. How will you stay motivated during your career search?

YOU CAN DO IT

Now you have the tools it takes for the job you want. But the opportunity you seek will take hard work, determination, and a positive attitude. Circumstances and people may get you down. The road to your new job may become bumpy, but you can do it! For some final inspiration, here are some quotations to keep in mind.

"Keep your face to the sunshine and you cannot see the shadows."
- Helen Keller -

"It's not whether you get knocked down, it's whether you get up."
- Vince Lombardi -

"If opportunity doesn't knock, build a door."
- Milton Berle -

"Do something for somebody every day for which you do not get paid."
- Albert Schweitzer -

"In the middle of difficulty lies opportunity."
- Albert Einstein -

"Far and away the best prize that life offers is the chance to work hard at work worth doing."
- Theodore Roosevelt -

"Only those who risk going too far can possibly find out how far one can go."
- T. S. Eliot -

"All our dreams can come true—if we have the courage to pursue them."
- Walt Disney -

"What lies behind us and what lies before us are tiny matters compared to what lies within us."
- Oliver Wendell Holmes -

INDEX